Growing Orchids at Your Windows

Growing

ORCHIDS
at Your Windows

by JACK KRAMER

Drawings and Photographs by
Andrew R. Addkison

HAWTHORN BOOKS, INC.
PUBLISHERS / New York

Library of Congress Catalog Card Number: 77-179120
ISBN: 0–8015–3175–6

3 4 5 6 7 8 9 10

Preface

BOTANICAL ORCHIDS AT MY WINDOWS

Not so long ago the idea of growing orchids in the home, and without a greenhouse, was considered almost as outlandish as flying to the moon. We know now that orchids can be more easily grown than many house plants and that soon there will be flights to the moon, too. Those who see the orchid plants I have collected in my apartment in the last eight years are always amazed at the beauty and quantity of the flowers on what are actually house plants, and they invariably ask, "Can I really grow these in my home?" I tell them of course they can, just as I have.

Fallacious theories about orchid growing started years ago when the first plants were brought to England. The orchids were immediately enclosed in tight glass structures or placed in greenhouses with high heat and humidity. Eventually most of the plants died. This did not discourage fanciers; it only made prices higher and plants scarce. From that time to this, orchid culture has come a long way.

In the 1930's, many apartment buildings in large cities were constructed with sun porches or solariums, as they were called, and these were usually located at the rear of the dwellings. In my apartment, the sunroom is at the front adjoining the living room but separated by doors. This is an extra room for me and my first thought was to fill it with green plants. It is on the west side of the house and gets only four hours of sun a day so I didn't for a moment think of this porch as a place for orchids, though I had been wanting to try them for some time. The people and books I had consulted on culture all stipulated hours and hours of sun, an essential southern exposure, high humidity, and various other difficult requirements. I suspected they were wrong, yet I hesitated to meet the challenge until I received two Cattleya plants as a gift. That was all I needed. I threw out my philodendrons and oleanders and I launched into this fascinating hobby of orchids.

In general my information on culture added up to this: 1. Not much water; 2. Not much repotting; 3. Not much cold. Everything wrong, I found out later, for growing orchids at home.

Heating arrangements bothered me most. There were only two radiators on the porch, one at each end. So my jungle plants were going to be at the mercy of my landlord's blood pressure, which at times isn't too good. For the summer there was no problem, I had an open back porch. But in winter in the Midwest it gets very cold. Still, I decided to give orchids a try and started hunting for plants in the florist shops. I felt a little like grandma with her African violets, which, incidentally, are far trickier to raise than orchids, I have discovered. It seemed to me that each florist looked at me a little more skeptically than the one before. From florists I went to wholesale growers and finally to seed-and-bulb shops but with no luck. Then I discovered not far away an orchid grower with a fair-sized greenhouse of Cattleya plants. But he was reluctant to sell to me when he learned I had no greenhouse. At last I came upon a pamphlet on orchid growing with a list of suppliers. In a month I had five pots of Cattleyas, but I was sure there was more to the orchid family than these familiar corsage flowers. And how right I was! I discovered the botanicals or species—those orchids that are pure from the hand of Nature. They are her own invention, as are some of the crosses or hybrids, though many of these are the result of the intervention of man. I found that the botanical orchids would bloom for me at home as well as they did in nature. And more exotic flowers cannot be found. Nor more unusual plants. There are small ones and big ones with blooms of a brilliance to surpass the majestic Cattleya hybrids. Flowers of some look like moths, others resemble pansies or spiders or frogs and some suggest lilacs and have as lovely a perfume. To me, these were tremendously exciting plants. The botanicals come from all over the world—South America, Panama, Guatemala, Honduras, Malaya, India, China and Africa. I decided to tackle any I could find except the Cattleyas. The material on these is ample but, while there is some technical data on the botanicals, general information is scarce.

My notes on culture are not meant to be rules, only suggestions. The treatment outlined has worked for me under my conditions, and I hope it will work for you. Under your conditions, some modification may be necessary. Your common sense plus my suggestions, however, should add up to successful orchid culture in your house. Size of flowers and color also may vary for you, and this should be expected. But no matter where you grow orchids, I can promise you that once you start, there's no cure.

I suggest you join the American Orchid Society where you can meet other enthusiasts. Membership will bring you the American Orchid Society's *Bulletin*, a magazine full of pertinent information. It is not sold on newsstands. For more information write to the American Orchid Society, Inc., Botanical Museum of Harvard University, Cambridge 38, Massachusetts.

You will find that my book is not a technical discussion by any means, but a detailed first-hand account of the more than 100 plants I have grown and flowered in my city apartment, and a few of the tricks and accommodations I have learned along the way.

J. K.

Chicago, Illinois

Contents

Illustrations

Photographs

1 THE BUYING
OF PLANTS

Orchids can be called the flower of four seasons for there are orchids that bloom in spring, summer, autumn, and winter, and it is a good idea to collect your plants with this in mind. You can have as few as four or six plants and still have bloom just about all year round. The winter months, especially dull and gray in the Midwest, abound with the flowers of the Mormodes, the Miltonias, Odontoglossums, Oncidiums, Cycnoches, Coelogynes, and others. For spring, there are the amazing Dendrobiums, Calanthes, and Aspasias, just to mention a few, and in the summer, the Brassias, Brassavolas and Epidendrums come into flower, and so on and on. Then there are the miniature orchids and the really rare ones for collectors. There are thousands! You need to know the nature of each species you acquire in order to grow it properly.

COST OF PLANTS

The cost of orchid plants is not exorbitant: a good-sized specimen will be four to seven dollars. I have only four plants

1

for which I paid more than ten dollars, and these are actually collector's items. Enough reasonably priced botanicals are available to content you for years. For the most part, you can obtain your plants from local dealers or from mail-order houses. Try always, even if it costs a little more, to secure mature plants, that is plants that have already flowered. You can usually see the remains of the last year's flower spike still on the plant.

A mature plant is best because it has a good chance of surviving in an apartment or house. Seedlings are not for the home hobbyist. Also, I don't think jungle plants, that is orchids direct from the source, are a good investment either. They are cheaper, true, but have a tough time getting adjusted to the home conditions they must accept. Furthermore, they are always shipped bare root and so need a good deal of attention and time right at the start.

If you do decide to import orchids direct from a foreign source, you will have to obtain a plant permit. For information, write to Permit Unit, Plant Quarantine Division, 209 River Street, Hoboken, New Jersey. There is no charge for the service.

SOURCES OF PLANTS

As a rule, I buy from mail-order orchid specialists throughout the country, and I stipulate plants that are potted and well established. I prefer to buy in nearby Indiana, Wisconsin, Michigan, or the East. Plants from these areas are already accustomed to a climate similiar to that here in the Midwest. I have found this makes quite a difference in the success of a plant. Specimens from northern California and Washington also do well for me, but plants from Florida and other warm states are slow to adjust to my conditions. I do not suggest that plants from the South are inferior, only that it is harder for them to come around when they are moved to this climate of severe winter cold.

When plants arrive, I soak them in a sink of warm water, right up to the pot rims, for half an hour or so. This treatment gets rid of any insects that the potting bark may harbor and, if the supplier is new to me, I isolate his plant for a few days so as to take no chances with my collection as a whole. Most plants come in bark or osmunda, and these offer the most satisfactory media. You might get some plants in hapu (Mexican tree fern) pumice stone, or charcoal, or some other recently derived material, but by and large, bark is preferred and "osmundine" acceptable.

Beware of bargains and plant dividends and too-low prices. Usually, these are inferior specimens collected in the jungle and pushed out for fast sale. They rarely if ever prove themselves and are just not worth your trouble. If you are so fortunate as to have an orchid source near you, do go to the greenhouse to select your own plants. This way you can know what you are buying, and also the local plant has a better chance to succeed. Orchids are durable and hard to kill but no one wants plants that will not bloom. Purchasing mature healthy specimens of your own selection will give you a head start towards flowering them.

Seasonal Bloom on Imports

The natural flowering time of plants is also a factor in your success. Sometimes plants imported from a part of the world where the seasons are opposite to ours as in South America, arrive in winter with a flowering spike already visible. Here their natural flowering time would be spring. I have found that if I allow such plants to bloom that first winter, they of course do not flower that spring, or as a matter of fact, the next spring. They will thus skip two flowering years. To avoid this, I cut off the flower spike, unhappily to be sure, but this does work out better for the plant. Then the plant reverts to a natural cycle for this country. To learn just what the normal blooming time is for a species, I consult Sander's *Orchid Guide* or Williams' *The Orchid Growers Manual*, and give my new plant rest periods and light according to the recommendations in these guides.

Your First Selection

What characteristics do you prefer in orchid species? Many of the botanicals are spray orchids, and it is not unusual to have fifty or a hundred tiny flowers opening on a branch at one time. Some bloom in clusters; others are single-flowered. Generally orchids bloom only once a year, like *Cattleya forbesii* and *Lycaste aromatica*. But some species, like *Miltonia roezlii* and *Coelogyne massangeana*, when well grown, bloom more than once. There are also some like *Epidendrum o'brienianum* and *Brassavola nodosa* that are in flower most of the time. You will find that in their first year with you some orchids will give you only one or two flowers but the next year when they are established in your home, they will come back a little stronger with four or five flowers.

Don't be too concerned about the appearance of your plants. Some like *Oncidium splendidum* and *Chysis laevis* look notoriously poor when out of bloom. But there are others like *Aspasia principissa* and *Brassia maculata* that are always handsome foliage plants. Most botanicals do not resemble the Cattleya corsage flower as we know it, and at first you may find it hard to believe that your plants are true orchids.

Each month new and fascinating species are being discovered, and these, in time, will be available to you. And yet in spite of the tremendous variety of botanicals available for you to grow at your windows, the surface of the possibilities has hardly been scratched.

Here are six easy orchids that I recommend for your first selection. Each is fully described and illustrated in Chapter 5.

Cycnoches chlorochilon
Brassavola nodosa
Lycaste aromatica
Odontoglossum grande
Oncidium sarcodes
Stanhopea oculata

2 WHERE TO PLACE YOUR ORCHID PLANTS

Whether you have a few orchid plants or many, whether you grow them on a window sill or elsewhere, common sense will play a great part in your success or failure. You will find that plants indicate their needs to you, and I hope through this book you will be able to recognize these needs. For orchids, their position in life is not everything, but it is important.

Because orchids have diversified light requirements, any window in any room can easily be made into a growing area for some of them. But plants should not be placed directly on window sills or floors since *bottom ventilation is absolutely necessary*. Some of my first orchids were set on redwood strips over standard clay saucers, as in Figure 1. Later I used redwood strips over galvanized metal trays as shown in Figure 2. These trays are inexpensive and sheet-metal houses will make them to size for you. They can be set on aquarium stands or on any table or box that will put them at window-sill height and close enough to the glass to receive light. Metal refrigera-

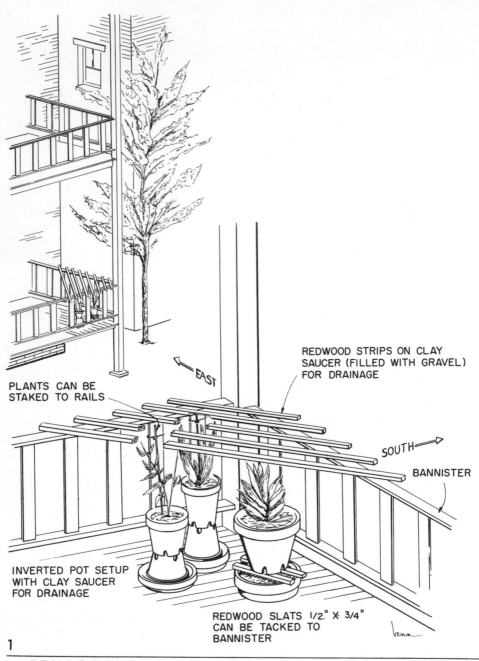

REDWOOD STRIPS ON CLAY
SAUCER (FILLED WITH GRAVEL)
FOR DRAINAGE

EAST

PLANTS CAN BE
STAKED TO RAILS

SOUTH

BANNISTER

INVERTED POT SETUP
WITH CLAY SAUCER
FOR DRAINAGE

REDWOOD SLATS 1/2." X 3/4"
CAN BE TACKED TO
BANNISTER

1

TEMPORARY LATH HOUSE FOR CORNER OF OUTSIDE PORCH

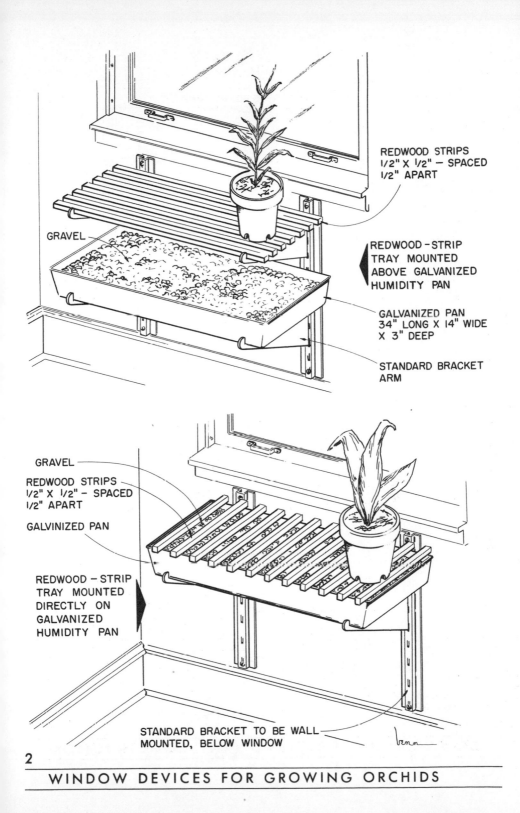

REDWOOD STRIPS
1/2" X 1/2" — SPACED
1/2" APART

GRAVEL

REDWOOD-STRIP
TRAY MOUNTED
ABOVE GALVANIZED
HUMIDITY PAN

GALVANIZED PAN
34" LONG X 14" WIDE
X 3" DEEP

STANDARD BRACKET
ARM

GRAVEL

REDWOOD STRIPS
1/2" X 1/2" — SPACED
1/2" APART

GALVINIZED PAN

REDWOOD-STRIP
TRAY MOUNTED
DIRECTLY ON
GALVANIZED
HUMIDITY PAN

STANDARD BRACKET TO BE WALL
MOUNTED, BELOW WINDOW

2

WINDOW DEVICES FOR GROWING ORCHIDS

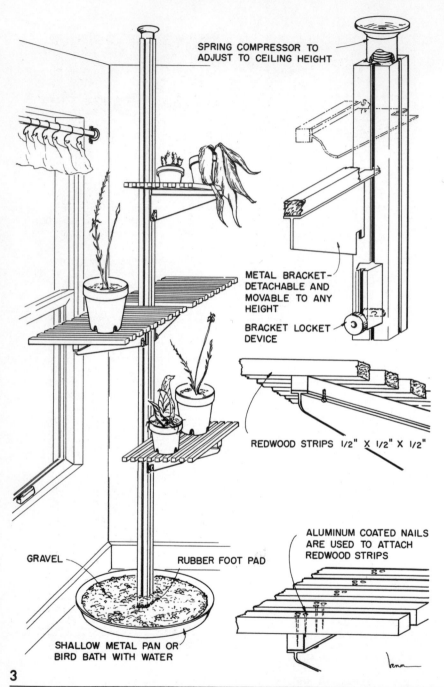

SPRING COMPRESSOR TO
ADJUST TO CEILING HEIGHT

METAL BRACKET-
DETACHABLE AND
MOVABLE TO ANY
HEIGHT

BRACKET LOCKET
DEVICE

REDWOOD STRIPS 1/2" X 1/2" X 1/2"

ALUMINUM COATED NAILS
ARE USED TO ATTACH
REDWOOD STRIPS

GRAVEL

RUBBER FOOT PAD

SHALLOW METAL PAN OR
BIRD BATH WITH WATER

3

SPACE-SAVING POLE-AND-TRAY CONSTRUCTION

1   Orchid Plants on Pole Shelves at Windows in a Sun Porch

tor or oven shelves can be used instead of redwood strips, and baking tins or trays can be substituted for made-to-order trays.

My own arrangement now consists of a pole-type shelf construction shown in Figure 3 and Photo 1. The aluminum poles are 2 inches square and are designed for book case or partition use. They do not attach to floor or ceiling (no problem with landlords), but are secured by spring compressors. These poles have detachable brackets that can be adjusted to any desired height. The shelves for the brackets are made from half-inch redwood strips with half-inch air spaces between. Each shelf is 12 inches square and accommodates two plants. Six, seven, or even eight brackets can be used with one pole so at one window of your home you can grow twelve or sixteen plants. These poles are available at most department stores.

WINDOW GREENHOUSES

Greenhouses that extend beyond your window are also available and come with do-it-yourself construction sheets. I have seen these and I think they might be excellent for orchids, but at present they are expensive and hardly needed at the start of your hobby. Enclosed glass cases and plastic growing boxes are also on the market as well as the old-type Wardian cases. I do not recommend a tightly-enclosed case for growing orchids.

A friend of mine grows her plants on wood slats over pie plates on a movable tea cart. In winter, they are in her bedroom at a south window; in summer, they are moved to an east window in her recreation room. In essence, she follows the sun and her plants benefit greatly from it.

I have also seen living-room arrangements of planter boxes filled with orchid plants and quite elaborate plantings for bay windows and sun porches. Cattleya species and some Dendrobiums love the warmth and humidity of a kitchen window. I have seen Coelogyne and Stanhopea species flourishing in bathrooms in front of dim windows where they receive diffused south light, very beneficial to these plants. These are only a few suggestions of ways to accommodate orchids in your home. There are many possibilities and how you will manage depends on your space and pocketbook.

At House Windows

Most orchid plants bloom well with four hours of direct morning or afternoon sun, but there are some genera that need shade and some that require a few hours of filtered sunlight. Angraecums, Arachnis, and most Renantheras and Vandas require a full eight hours of direct sunshine and are not for the home grower. If your available space is at a south window, I suggest you try species from the Cattleya, Dendrobium, Oncidium, and Brassia families. At an east window, most Brassavolas and Laelias and hard-bulb Oncidiums will do well. At west windows, Coelogynes and Pleiones and Gongoras will be right at home. And for the orphan north exposure, there is the Stanhopea family and a great many Coelogynes.

South and east windows in mild, temperate climates need some shading. Screens will help, or you can draw a thin curtain at midday.

Under Fluorescent Lights

If tall buildings or other obstructions limit sunlight, you can still grow orchids under fluorescent lights specifically designed for plants. This idea is not new. Greenhouse men have been using such light to lengthen days for many commercial crops. Amateurs have installed fluorescent tubes for African violets and various foliage plants. Now the Gro-Lux fluorescent tube combines both the red and the blue of the spectrum to make "sunshine." These tubes come in lengths of 18 to 96 inches. They supply invaluable supplemental sunlight in climates where winters are gray and the sun sometimes does not shine for days at a stretch. Gro-Lux tubes can be fitted over homemade well-ventilated glass cases or terrariums or even above partitions with planter boxes that are away from windows. Table models and movable wagons with reflective canopies are available. With these, all you need do is install the Gro-Lux tubes.

Fluorescent lighting has opened new avenues for hobbyists. Useless basement space is now blossoming with orchids as well as attics and various dim areas. Users of artificial lighting in the home report stronger plants and more blossoms. As a rule, plants grown under lights are summered out-of-doors. A few months outside with natural air currents, rain water, and sun keep plants in top condition.

I am inclined to feel that supplemental artificial lighting in the home offers the amateur a better method of growing plants than a greenhouse. Most greenhouses are at ground level and subject to some insect invasions. Ventilation is always a problem as well as shading, not to mention the cost of heating and water systems. None of these is present in home culture.

Photoperiodism and Orchids

I recently installed a tray-and-cart arrangement with Gro-Lux tubes; I use it as a supplement on gray winter days. I am also trying a few test plants to study photoperiodism, the response of plants to day-length. This is an interesting subject but still in its infancy with orchids. We know that certain Cattleya, Phalaenopsis, and Cypripedium species favor short days and longer nights, to initiate buds. Other species bloom only with long-day light and short nights.

Closely allied to the effect of day-length is temperature. Each species has to be considered by itself, for at this time we know few rules about temperature that are all-inclusive. If some of your plants fail to blossom, it may be a question of day-length. If you have artificial lighting, you can experiment.

3 HOW TO GROW ORCHIDS IN YOUR HOME

Contrary to general opinion, orchids are not parasites, although many are *air plants* or *epiphytes*. In nature, they grow mainly lodged in trees or bushes but derive no direct nourishment from these. It is the rain washing down the minerals that helps keep orchids alive. Plants use trees only for footholds.

There are also botanical orchids that grow in soil, as most plants do. These are called *terrestrials*. Despite such marked differences in habit, both types of orchid plants thrive in the home.

PREFERRED TEMPERATURES

Average home temperatures of 56 to 62 degrees F. at night in winter, and 62 to 80 degrees F. during the day, will suit most orchids. Cool-growing genera of Odontoglossum and Miltonia need 6 to 10 degrees cooler, and warm groups, such as some Oncidiums and Dendrobiums need 6 to 10 degrees warmer. However, a great many orchids prove adaptable, and it is an easy matter to place cool growers a little closer to the window where the temperature will be lower in winter, or warm growers back from the window where it will be higher. And usually there is one room in your house that is a little cooler or warmer than the others. If you have your own thermostat there is no problem. When you are comfortable, many of the orchids will be, too. Coal or gas heat or radiant baseboard heating will not harm orchid plants.

In many places, hot summer months are unavoidable unless you have air conditioning. If you lack this facility, as I do, try to keep the humidity high on very warm days. A few 90- to 100-degree days will not kill your orchids.

I find that circulation of air is more important to success with orchids than almost any other factor since most of them are air plants. I run two small electric fans at low speed in hot weather to provide a gentle movement of air in the growing area, but directed away from the plants. In winter, one fan remains on to keep air moving. Generally, the fans are shut off at night unless the room seems stuffy.

Plants respond poorly to sudden changes of temperature and to drafts. When you ventilate, open windows other than those beside them and thus freshen the atmosphere indirectly.

When to Water

Watering orchids in the home is different from greenhouse watering. If winter heat fluctuates, so must the home-watering schedule. The more artificial heat dries out the air, the more water the plants will need.

Size of pots also affects watering. Small pots dry out quickly, large pots slowly. Clay pots dry out fast, plastic pots take longer. The type of compost is a factor too. Fir bark dries out faster than osmunda. If a pot feels light when you pick it up, it generally means the compost is dry and should be watered. If it feels heavy in your hand, wait to water. Some growers put a thin layer of sphagnum or peat moss over the surface of the potting material. When this dries out, they water. If you are in doubt, don't water. It is important to use tepid water of about 60 to 70 degrees; no plant likes to be shocked with ice cold water. In time you will be able to judge each plant's requirement, but I don't believe it is possible to follow a watering schedule that will suit all your plants.

How Much Humidity

High humidity is not necessary for orchids in the home or in a greenhouse. When I started growing orchids, the humidity around my plants was 30 to 40 percent. With a space humidifier, which I rarely use in summer, I found I could increase humidity to 50 to 70 percent. However, such constant high humidity would be harmful. Orchids do better with lower humidity along with a lower temperature at night; some species do need high humidity, but these are the exceptions rather than the rule. Humidity will vary depending on where you live, and there are always ways to increase or reduce it artificially. Particular needs of particular plants are indicated in Chapter 5.

If you are using galvanized trays with gravel or gravel-filled saucers, a certain amount of humidity will be provided by the evaporation of the excess water draining from the plants. Misting the air around the plants will increase humidity for a few hours, and the old-fashioned method of pans of water on radiators has its uses, too. Daily misting or spraying is necessary on sunny days in spring and summer. In autumn and winter, this is only necessary, say, once a week.

There are a number of mist and spray guns on the market but I use a fifteen-cent window-cleaning bottle and find it quite satisfactory. Avoid directing mist or spray onto your plants, and spray if possible early in the day. Orchids are susceptible to disease if water remains overnight on foliage or in the crowns of plants. If you have many plants growing together, they themselves will create additional humidity.

Houses are now being built with humidifiers as part of the furnace operation. And room-size plastic lightweight space humidifiers are now available. These operate with a small inside fan and a motor that breaks up water particles into a fine mist. An hygrometer to measure air moisture is a real help.

TYPES OF POTS

Most orchids can be potted in the slotted clay pots made expressively for the orchid industry. However, standard clay pots can be used if you will gently hammer out and enlarge the drainage hole. Pot sizes are chosen according to genus. Dendrobium, Lycaste, and Miltonia, because of their compact pseudobulbs do best in 4- or 5-inch pots; Laelia, Oncidium, and Cattleya require large pots, unless they are dwarf species. Proper pot sizes are suggested in the descriptions of the plants in Chapter 5.

Available now are attractive ceramic containers designed with air holes and spaces on the sides. There are hanging types, too. Of course, these decorative containers cost more than standard slotted clay pots.

Plastic lightweight pots are also acceptable for many orchid species.

Bottomless baskets of cedar or redwood are excellent for many orchids, as the Stanhopeas, Gongoras, and Acinetas. All of these produce pendant flower spikes that in some cases grow straight down so plants must be potted in baskets. Angraecum, Vanda, and Phalaenopsis species with their long aerial roots do well in baskets, too. It is not necessary to use broken pot pieces in the bottom of baskets to facilitate drainage since the containers themselves have open spaces. Baskets can be set on window trays or suspended by wires from the ceiling. But when you water, the excess water will drip on the floor unless a clay saucer or pie plate is placed there to catch it.

Small orchids, like those of the Cirrhopetalum and Bulbophyllum species, and most miniature types of Oncidiums and Epidendrums thrive on oval slabs of compressed tree fern or pieces of cork bark available from orchid-supply houses. In fact, the majority of miniature plants should be treated in this manner. Any coarse-bark tree is an excellent host, too.

Long wire baskets from variety stores, actually made for draining silverware, are perfect containers for rambling-rhizome plants like some species of Coelogynes and the larger Bulbophyllums. These do well potted tight in osmunda. I have recently transferred many of my orchids to such containers. In these there is no danger of overwatering since the compost is always visible for examination. A visit to the pots-and-pans section of any department store may give you other ideas.

POTTING MIXTURES

Many potting materials have been used for orchids. Osmunda fiber has proven satisfactory through the years. Fir bark is now very popular. Pumice stone and charcoal have been used, too. I cannot suggest an ideal compost; I don't think it has been found yet. Each kind has advantages as well as disadvantages. I pot many orchids in fir bark: the bark of the Douglas or white fir tree that has been graded into chunks of varying size and then steamed. I add some sphagnum or peat moss for the Aspasias and Bifrenarias that seem to need constant moisture at the roots. For the Cattleyas and Trichopilias that require complete drying out between waterings, I add shredded tree fern known as hapu. Prepared bark is available in small, medium, and large pieces. If you use fir bark, be sure to sift out particles that are sometimes mixed in during processing. If these remain, they may clog drainage.

Osmunda fiber or osmundine is the fibrous aerial root of two types of osmunda fern. This fiber holds water, dries out slowly over a long period, and has space between the fibers to permit circulation of air. As the material decays, usually in two to three years, it releases mineral nutrients vital for growth. Although more difficult to pot with than fir bark, it does have advantages.

Terrestrial and semi-terrestrial orchids, such as the Calanthe and Pleione families, are better potted in a mixed compost of one part humus, one part chopped osmunda or sphagnum moss, and one part leaf mold.

How to Pot Orchid Plants

All potting materials must be absolutely clean. I wash and scrub pots and broken pieces of pot in scalding water. When you remove a plant from a pot, try not to force or pull it out. Pressure can damage live roots. Instead gently tap the outside of the pot with a hammer and gradually tease the plant out of the old mixture. Then carefully clean away all old compost from around the roots and cut off any shriveled dead roots (Figure 4).

Fill the new pot one-half to one-third with broken pieces of pot or shards as they are called. Set the plant in place and fill in with fresh bark, occasionally pressing it down with a blunt-edged potting stick or piece of wood. Always work from the sides of the pot to the center until you have filled up to within half an inch of the rim. Stake the plant if necessary with wire or wooden sticks and label it. Most orchids require tight hard potting; a few are better loosely planted and this will be discussed under each species. Some growers recommend the use of wet bark, that is, bark first soaked overnight. But I use dry bark and it proves satisfactory.

Potting with osmunda takes more time (Figure 5). Since the compost is hard and dry, it should be soaked overnight in water so it will be easier to handle. Remove the plant from the old pot as suggested and fill the new pot with drainage pieces. Then with a sharp knife cut the osmunda into chunks about 3 inches square. Set the plant in the pot and fill in around it with chunks of osmunda. With a potting stick, push these down rather hard toward the center of the pot. Trim away any excess at the surface.

When you are potting with fir bark or osmunda, make certain of good drainage so essential to healthy growth. Excess moisture at the root ball means disaster. In fact, more orchids are killed by overwatering than by any other error of culture, and this would not occur if they had been potted properly.

If you are using slabs of tree fern or tree branches that you

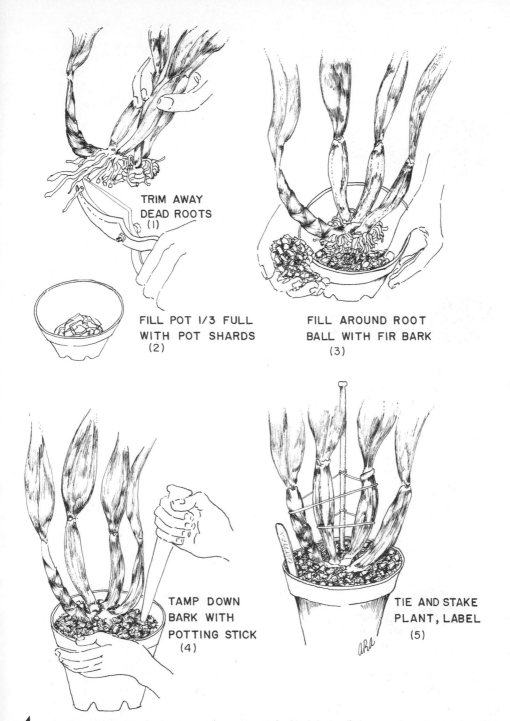

TRIM AWAY
DEAD ROOTS
(1)

FILL POT 1/3 FULL
WITH POT SHARDS
(2)

FILL AROUND ROOT
BALL WITH FIR BARK
(3)

TAMP DOWN
BARK WITH
POTTING STICK
(4)

TIE AND STAKE
PLANT, LABEL
(5)

POTTING WITH FIR BARK

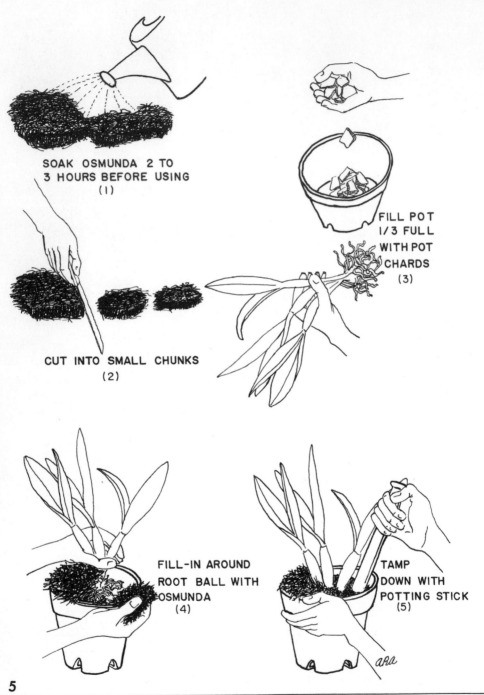

SOAK OSMUNDA 2 TO
3 HOURS BEFORE USING
(1)

CUT INTO SMALL CHUNKS
(2)

FILL POT
1/3 FULL
WITH POT
CHARDS
(3)

FILL-IN AROUND
ROOT BALL WITH
OSMUNDA
(4)

TAMP
DOWN WITH
POTTING STICK
(5)

POTTING WITH OSMUNDA

yourself have cut for plants, gently wrap the root ball in damp osmunda. With a piece of string or galvanized wire, tie the root ball to the slab or branch and leave it for a few weeks until roots have taken hold. Then cut off the strings or wire.

After the potting or repotting, it is a good idea to place plants in a moderately warm temperature of 60 to 78 degrees and out of direct sun. *Do not water.* Wait at least seven to ten days, even two to three weeks, before watering. Instead, daily spray the immediate area around the plants with a very fine mist of water; misting the pot and the very edge of the surface of the compost is all right too. But never spray water directly on the foliage or bulbs of a newly potted orchid.

When to Fertilize

Fir bark is deficient in nitrogen so you must supplement with fertilizer. A 20-10-10 or a 10-5-5 formula (figures indicate percentages of nitrogen, phosphoric acid, potash) is excellent. Contents are plainly marked on the bottle and the mixtures can be purchased at florist shops. When a plant is in active growth, make applications about every ten to fourteen days. Time of growth varies with the individual species; for some plants, it will be spring and summer; others, autumn and winter.

Many species react adversely to heavy feeding so fertilize with care. Too much nitrogen can prevent flowering. You may have to try different brands of fertilizers to check reactions under your conditions. Once every month, in winter too, a weak application of Atlas Fish Emulsion has proved beneficial for my plants.

Plants in osmunda require little if any additional feeding. If they are in active growth, about once every five weeks is enough, and none at all during autumn and winter.

Ways to Promote Bloom

Keep a careful eye on your orchid plants for poor growth. If the leaves of a plant start to turn yellow, check the amount of water you are giving and the possibility of too much sun. If the compost or bark stays soggy, stop watering altogether. Then if it is moist after seven or eight days, remove the plant from the pot. Do not immediately repot. Instead, I wrap the plant loosely in newspaper and put it in a cooler place, about 60 degrees, where there is good air circulation. In a day or two, I pot it again as usual.

If a plant falls from stand or window tray, don't throw it away. Trim the bruised or cracked areas with a sterilized knife (I use a pocketknife) and repot.

To the eye, an orchid plant may appear completely dormant for months of the year. No root activity, no green leads, nothing is in evidence. Don't try to force growth under these conditions. When the plant is ready to grow, you will see the signs—a fresh white root or a tiny green shoot.

There are cases where a plant fails to respond even under the best culture. I believe this is because it is a weak specimen that cannot adjust to the necessary change of environment. If I have space, I keep it, otherwise, out it goes.

When a plant refuses to bloom although it has had proper culture, it may need a different day-length. If you have fluorescent lights, you can experiment with different amounts of light and the plant may bloom. Otherwise, as I have said, hope for the best; it is not possible to be a hundred percent successful in flowering orchids. Even light reflected from across the street and quite far away can have an effect. For some orchids, five- to ten-foot candles, can make a difference, though they don't contribute much light really. I had a Cattleya species that did not bloom for two years, not even a hint of a bud. I moved it to the floor away from the glare of the street lamps at night and it blossomed the same year.

Let flowers stay on a plant for two to three days before you cut them. It takes this long for color and form fully to develop. When you cut, use a sterilized knife. I run a match flame over the blade for a few seconds. The heat also seals the cut stem.

Possible Pests and Diseases

When I started growing orchids at home, I expected the plants to be plagued with insects. Since they are housed directly off my bedroom and living room, I was naturally concerned. I know now how mistaken I was about orchid pests. I have had almost no trouble. Only very occasionally have I found a snail, slug, or sowbug that came on the bark of a new plant. From time to time a plant may be attacked by mealy bugs or red spider. Since I check my orchids daily, pot by pot—and you too will fall into this habit as you watch for new buds or green leads—cleaning up trouble is easy. The first step is to isolate the attacked plants so pests cannot spread through your collection. Then give the proper treatment.

Chewing insects include ants, weevils, Cattleya fly, slugs, snails, sowbugs, and springtails. Their work is easily seen. Sucking pests, scale, thrips, mealy bugs, red spider, draw out the juices of a plant. D-X Aero-Spray bomb is easy to use and controls most of these pests. Super-Cide containing DDT and rotenone and pyrethrum is also a good all-purpose insecticide. Malathion is effective but it has an obnoxious smell so I do not use it. A liquid preparation called Last Bite, with 50 percent metaldehyde is effective on slugs and snails, as is Slugit, an English preparation. All of these are available from most orchid-supply houses and at some hardware stores.

If fungus appears, and I have had only one case of this, I try Natriphene (sold by orchid-supply house). I soak the plant, pot and all, in a bucket of the solution for half an hour, and repeat this twice a week for two weeks. If this does not cure the ailment, I discard the plant. I do not try to cope with virus diseases. If leaves develop spots with concentric rings or fine streaks of black or red watery areas, I discard the plant. Virus diseases in orchid plants are still very much a mystery.

As a routine preventative, I spray with an insecticide every fifth week in spring and summer. In autumn, only once, and through the winter not at all. My orchids are housed on the second floor of an apartment building and perhaps this is why I've had so little trouble. In greenhouses at ground level and under crowded conditions, I imagine it is more difficult to keep plants healthy. In any case, catching trouble before it starts is the secret, I think.

4 SUMMERING PLANTS OUTDOORS

Many apartments have an open back porch, and this is an ideal place for many orchids in summer. The increased sunlight along with rainfall and natural air currents does wonders for plants that have been indoors for many months. Any of the Cattleyas, Oncidiums, Epidendrums, Vandas, Brassias, Angraecums, Dendrobiums, and Brassavolas will benefit from outdoor conditions.

A PORCH LATH-HOUSE

In the corner of my porch, I build a rough lath-house. I use 1 x 2 redwood boards and set them diagonally across the bannister, as shown in Figure 1, page 6. Only six or seven boards are needed. You don't want to close off the area entirely since you need access to it to water the plants. The boards I use are set on the railings but they can be nailed on if you prefer. Space them 1 inch apart so they will break the direct sunshine.

In June, when it seems likely the weather will stay warm, I put a few plants outside. At first, I watch them closely. The sudden exposure to outside sun may burn the foliage; if this occurs, I put the boards closer together. It's a good idea to set the plants on inverted pots with a large clay saucer underneath to catch dripping water. (Otherwise it will run down onto your neighbor's porch if you are above the first floor.) By keeping pots off the wood floor, crawling insects are discouraged from entering the fir bark or osmunda. To prevent high winds from knocking over plants, staking is necessary. You can solve this problem by tying plants to the railing with string or tie-ons (available at florist shops).

Outside, watering depends on rainfall. I place my plants close to the edge of the porch. Even though there is a roof there, slanting rain reaches them. In dry, hot summer weather, I water plants every day for they dry out quickly in the open air. Occasional misting around the lath-house area is also beneficial. I spray with an all-purpose insecticide once a week and fertilize every ten days.

In late September, or whenever the weather starts to turn cool and night temperatures are around 58 degrees, I take plants inside with the exception of the deciduous Dendrobiums and some Odontoglossums and Oncidiums. The Dendrobes remain until the end of October for temperatures of 40 to 50 degrees do wonders for these orchids. One year I left two plants of *Dendrobium nobile* outside until late November when temperatures were around freezing. These amazed me next spring with a brilliant display of flowers.

In Garden or Patio

In year-round warm climates there are many ways to accommodate orchids outside. A friend in southern Florida attaches plants to trees in his back yard. They stay there all year even when the temperature occasionally dips into the low forties. His collection is full of very healthy Brassias, Brassavolas, Cattleyas and Laelias. Trees, of course, are natural hosts and orchids will not injure them. A rough-bark tree

such as an oak is ideal. Sunlight filtering through the leaves is
beneficial to most orchids.

Although it is not difficult to place an orchid plant without a pot directly onto a tree branch, it does take time. Try to
get as much usable compost from the pot as you can and wrap
it and the roots of the plant in damp osmunda. Then tie thin
wire or string around the roots to keep them intact. If you
have a stapler, use this to fasten the osmunda-wrapped root
ball to the tree, stapling along the edges of the osmunda. If
this does not secure the plant to the tree, tap two galvanized
nails into the tree, one on each side of the root ball. Then
tie this to the nails with wire or string. If you don't have a
staple-gun, simply use the nail-and-wire method. In any case,
make sure the orchid plant is tight against the bark. It will
take from three months to a year for the orchid plant to
grow onto the tree.

If you prefer not to attach plants to a tree permanently,
suspend them in their pots from the branches with pot
hangers. This is perhaps best where the tree has heavy foliage.
Hang the orchids on low branches where morning and afternoon sun will strike the plants but they will be shaded from
intense midday sun. Follow the same watering procedure as
for orchids on a porch.

As Year-Round Garden Plants

In warm climates, it is possible to grow plants right in the
garden; there are many terrestrial orchids that will thrive in
garden soil. Cymbidiums are common in California and reed-
stemmed Epidendrums and Vandas and Renantheras are
often seen in Florida. The wonderful flowers of the Calanthes
and Phaius species are possibilities outside wherever temperatures do not go below freezing. Pleiones with their lovely
solitary blossoms are often found in regions of light snow
and can certainly be tried in the garden. Arachnis orchids
also make beautiful bedding plants. It is interesting to try
various species outside giving them the same conditions as
other garden plants but with special attention to drainage.

PLANTS AS DECORATION

Most orchid plants are decorative in the home or apartment, particularly Aspasias, Miltonias, and spray-type Oncidiums. There is rarely a time when I am not enjoying an orchid plant on my kitchen or dining table. At Christmas I move my Calanthes into the living room or reception hall where the pink or rose-colored flowers look very festive.

Orchid flowers last an amazingly long time on the plant. I have had Oncidium and Lycaste blooms stay fresh for five to seven weeks. Usually, I cut them off after about a month so as not to burden the plant and perhaps check next year's display. I water them sparingly, only about every fourth day.

AS CUT FLOWERS

Orchid flowers are a pleasure to cut. Some species are already perfectly "arranged"; just cut the stems. Spray-type Oncidiums and Epidendrums alone make lovely arrangements. Laelias in a small vase with a few appropriate green leaves for background are handsome, too. (Don't ever remove orchid leaves when you need additional foliage; this damages the plant.)

Lasting qualities of cut orchids vary. I had an *Oncidium sarcodes* that lasted seven weeks in a glass vase of water. Miltonias when cut are pretty but only good a few days off the plant, and Lycaste flowers fade so quickly they are not worth cutting.

The inflorescence of Phalaenopsis hybrids are magnificent as cut specimens. After several weeks, you can remove the spike and float the flowers in a bowl as you would gardenias or camellias. This way they freshen up considerably and last another week. Long spikes of cut Bletias are atractive in small containers and last about two weeks. Some of the Epidendrum orchids also last well when cut. Cattleya and dwarf Laelia species are lovely for small corsages, and many Oncidiums and Epidendrums are ideal for boutonnieres.

5 | 200 BEAUTIFUL ORCHIDS for YOU

A E R I D E S to V A N D A

AERIDES

Aerides is a genus of epiphytic orchids native to tropical Asia. They are handsome plants in flower and seem to do well in the home. Of the sixty species known, I have grown *Aerides odoratum, A. japonicum,* and *A. maculosum. Aerides fieldingii, A. multiflorum* and *A. crassifolium* are also worthwhile but a little difficult to locate. I think we will see more of these orchids in the near future.

The genus varies greatly in size. Some species are several feet tall, others are dwarf to about 12 inches. Without pseudobulbs, the plant has a central stem that carries fleshy evergreen leaves. In many species, thick clinging roots are produced between the leaf axils. The pendant spikes are axillary, with many close-set, usually scented flowers of waxy texture.

A. crassifolium, only 10 inches high, has amethyst-purple flowers. I have recently bought a fine plant of this species.

A. fieldingii, growing 2 to 3 feet, produces white flowers mottled with magenta with the lip stained purple.

29

A. japonicum is a miniature with leaves only 4 inches long and white flowers marked red, the lip spotted purple. *This Aerides is a perfect window plant and readily available now.*

A. maculosum is a stout dwarf plant with pale rose flowers spotted purple.

A. multiflorum, a dwarf variety, has many small rose flowers with darker spots on the lip.

A. odoratum, as the name implies, has a powerful but pleasing scent; the fragrance will fill your house. The small flowers are waxy-white blotched with pale magenta. This is a dependable plant and a good Aerides to start with.

Aerides require sunshine but not direct midday sun. Because they are intolerant of root disturbance, I let plants remain three to four years without repotting. Instead, I resurface pots with fresh compost at the time of new growth.

These orchids require moist conditions, temperatures of 62 to 78 degrees F. and at least 60 percent humidity through the warm summer months. In the growing season, spray a fine mist of water over the plants once a day. In winter, decrease watering but do not allow plants to get so dry that leaves shrivel.

ANOECTOCHILUS

Anoectochilus, a genus of mainly terrestrial orchids from tropical Asia and Malaya, is not grown for flowers but for the handsome foliage brightly marked with copper or gold or white. Called Jewel Orchids, about twenty species are known. Because they are so difficult, they are a constant challenge. The true Anoectochilus species are rare and expensive and I do not recommend them for the beginner. *Macodes, Goodyera, Haemaria, Enthyrodes,* and *Zeuzine,* once known as Anoectochilus because of their resemblance, are available and priced reasonably. I have grown *Haemaria discolor* and *Enthyrodes nobitis argyocentrum* with success. I have tried some of the others but they did not respond. Since most of them are very small plants, you might want to include a few in your collection and my failures may be your successes.

Most species are dwarf plants with broad leaves about 3 to 5 inches long. Without pseudobulbs, they have creeping rhizomes from which grow the leaf stems. The flowers come in erect spikes but are inconspicuous. Most authorities recommend cutting them off to promote the strength of the plant.

Haemaria discolor var. *dawsoniana* has green leaves with copper overtones and bright gold veins.

Enthyrodes nobitis argyocentrum produces silver-gray almost green leaves.

These foliage orchids need perfect drainage, a rich porous compost, temperatures of 72 to 80 degrees F. at all times, 70 percent humidity, protection from sun, no root disturbance, and no drafts. A friend who has been successful with this genus, grows her plants in an aquarium with a shallow layer of gravel in the bottom. This is kept fairly moist. The case is half covered with a pane of glass.

A large bell jar with the base cut out is also a possibility. Set three or four plants on a baking pan or pie plate covered with about 2 inches of gravel. Keep this slightly damp but *not wet*. Put the glass jar over the plants and leave the top open. Either device will maintain high humidity and warmth while preventing drafts.

Anoectochilus plants will come to you in 2- or 3-inch pots. Growing mixtures for this genus may vary considerably, but a compost of shredded osmunda and chopped sphagnum with some leaf mold suits most of them. Repot at signs of fresh growth. Work carefully to avoid even the slightest root damage. Water with discretion and treat each species as an individual. Like African violets, Jewel Orchids require patience and care based on close observation for success.

ASPASIA

Aspasia is a small genus native to Central and South America. Sometimes included with Odontoglossum and Miltonia, it really deserves, and now has, a classification of its own. Only two species are easily procured, *Aspasia principissa* and *A. epidendroides*. I have grown them but these are quite similar so you will not want to have both. The varieties *A. lunata* and *A. odorata* are different enough to be worthwhile but they are difficult to locate.

Aspasias have elongated compressed pseudobulbs about 4 inches long and evergreen, dark green, compact leathery foliage that grows 12 to 16 inches high. Even out of bloom they make handsome house plants. The delicate blossoms, clustered between the leaves, come in early spring; for me usually in March, and they last five to seven weeks.

A. principissa produces erect flower spikes 6 to 8 inches tall from the base of the pseudobulbs, emerging between them and the sheathing leaves. In the beginning, spikes and new buds are difficult to distinguish for they are the same dark green as the leaves. My plants were full of flower spikes before I actually noticed them. Flowers are 2 inches across, sepals and petals greenish, striped brown, the lip white with faint purple markings. The white turns yellow halfway through the flowering. At first I thought this was a sign of wilting but I know now that it is simply a natural tendency. Flowers have a fine spicy scent, fresh and pleasant.

On *A. epidendroides*, flowers are somewhat smaller and with more white in the coloring. The inflorescence of *A. lunata* and *A. odorata* is different, white spotted chocolate and the lip white with a violet blotch in the center.

Aspasias grow well in a shady position; direct sunlight should be avoided. I have potted these epiphytes in straight bark and in bark with a protective layer of sphagnum or

6

ASPASIA PRINCIPISSA

peat moss on the surface of the compost. This seems the better way, perhaps because it keeps the media warm and retains moisture longer. Tight or hard potting, too, is a good idea for these plants.

Intermediate temperature conditions suit this genus (56 to 68 degrees F. at night). Aspasias require considerable moisture during the growing season from spring to autumn. When the new growth has matured, decrease water and carry the plants on the dry side through the winter months but avoid complete drying out. After flowering and until new growth appears again curtail watering slightly.

BIFRENARIA

Bifrenarias with about a dozen species are epiphytes mainly native to Brazil and have been at times allied to the genus Lycaste. Although seldom seen in cultivation, they are handsome plants that produce large showy flowers. *Bifrenaria harrisoniae* and *B. tyrianthina* are the only two species that I have ever seen offered and they are similar in habit.

The genus is of dwarf, compact growth making the plants ideal where space is limited. They have four-angled pseudobulbs varying from 1 to 3 inches long with dark green, almost leathery leaves that rarely exceed 12 inches. Flowers appear in spring.

B. harrisoniae blooms on very short stout scapes, produced from the base of the pseudobulb. Usually there are just one or two flowers to a plant. The attractive cupped inflorescence is large, sometimes 3 inches across and appears clustered. Sepals and petals are big and fleshy, cream-white to yellow. The lip is reddish purple, slightly haired and marked with purple veins, streaked on the inside with red lines. Flowers last about three weeks on my plant.

B. tyrianthina makes a somewhat larger plant with large flowers of reddish purple, the lip colored with deeper veins.

BIFRENARIA HARRISONIAE

Grow Bifrenarias somewhat on the cool side (55 to 58 degrees F. at night in winter) and with two to three hours of filtered sun rather than direct sunshine during the day. I pot them in straight bark, medium grade, in 5- or 6-inch slotted clay pots and repot only every second year.

After Bifrenarias flower in late spring, encourage a short rest of three to five weeks, but do not allow the pseudobulbs to get dry enough to shrivel. If it is necessary, repot at this time. Once the new growth appears resume watering and increase the amount as growth develops. During the growing season keep the bark just evenly moist. Like their cousins the Lycastes, Bifrenarias are excellent plants to grow at a window.

BLETIA

Bletia is a genus with more than fifty species native to tropical America with a few from Brazil and Peru. They are related to the Phaius tribe and for the most part are terrestrial plants that once established bloom freely. *Bletia catenulata, B. gracilis, B. purpurea, B. shepherdii,* and *B. sherrattiana* all produce pretty, small, pink-to-rose flowers.

The species have round rather flat cormlike pseudobulbs and grassy, deciduous or nearly deciduous foliage 2 to 4 feet tall. The flower scapes come from the base of the bulb and are sometimes 3 feet tall, erect or arching under their own weight. For the most part, plants are deciduous and lose their leaves before flowering in spring or early summer. Blossoms are seldom long-lived but they are produced one after another so a plant can be in bloom for a long time, perhaps for seven to nine weeks.

B. catenulata has dark rose-colored flowers about 2 inches across with a strongly ridged lip making it very handsome.

B. gracilis produces 1- to 2-inch flowers pale purple or

8

BLETIA PURPUREA

purple-rose with a green lip veined dark red and purple; a striking plant.

B. purpurea is usually seen with six to twelve pink or rose flowers about 1½ inches across. They do not expand fully, and the petals form an open hood over the lip. This species is easier to grow than others in the genus and a good one to start with. It has done well for me.

B. shepherdii, also a success for me, is winter-flowering with slightly larger flowers, about 2½ inches across in pink or rose.

B. sherrattiana is perhaps the prettiest of the family but a little difficult to locate. The delicate textured flowers are large, showy, and rosy red, the lip dark purple with three yellow lines.

Bletias thrive in as much sun as you can provide in winter, but through the hot summer months place them at a west rather than a south or east window. Since they are terrestrial, provide a compost of leaf mold, sand, and fibrous loam. I have also tried commercial African violet soil and plants responded just as well. Do not completely cover the cormlike pseudobulbs but let about half an inch protrude above the compost. Make sure pots have ample drainage. I repot Bletias only when absolutely necessary but I do add fresh compost at the top from time to time.

Through the growing season plants require considerable water but when leaves start to fall decrease moisture somewhat and after flowering a bone-dry rest is essential. I put them in a slightly shaded place and leave them until I see signs of new growth, usually after six to eight weeks. Then I resume watering, moderately at first, and increased as growth develops.

Grow Bletias slightly cool (55 to 58 degrees F. at night in winter) and avoid a hot or stuffy atmosphere; a good circulation of air is essential.

Once in flower, plants can be moved anywhere in the house for decoration. The tall wandlike stems of pink flowers are most appealing and when cut they last a long time in water.

If you have trouble with this genus and plants do not respond, sacrifice the sunlight for shade and a cooler temperature. Plants then survive although they may not flower as well. Bletias are still not common in orchid collections but the family is rich in species and I'm sure we shall see more of them in the near future.

BRASSAVOLA

Brassavola is a genus of epiphytic orchids distributed mainly through Central America. It is not a spectacular family but a few species should be included in every collection. *Brassavola cucullata*, *B. nodosa*, *B. glauca*, and *B. digbyana*—all of which I have grown—are readily available and produce handsome white or greenish white flowers.

Most of the species have stemlike pseudobulbs topped by a solitary cactuslike leaf. The flowering time is variable, and healthy plants of *Brassavola cucullata* and *B. nodosa* sometimes blossom throughout the year. The flowers are scented and last two to three weeks on the plant.

B. nodosa, the "lady of the night" orchid, is famous for a delightful evening scent. This variety produces many large pale green flowers, sepals and petals narrow and elongated, lip scalloped.

B. cucullata, a small plant, is similar to *B. nodosa* and produces a larger flower, about 2 inches across, spotted with purple. Easy to grow and a perfect houseplant.

B. digbyana makes a somewhat larger plant often 2 feet tall and, although shy to bloom, the solitary flower is well worth waiting for. It is 6 inches across, pale green and with a handsomely fringed white lip. *This species is one of the most beautiful orchids grown.*

9

BRASSAVOLA GLAUCA

B. glauca is also a little reluctant to blossom. Not as large as *B. digbyana*, it produces a waxy textured white flower and although only one to a sheath, a healthy plant will have four or five flowers.

Brassavolas will tolerate more sunlight than most orchids and must have three to five hours of sunshine to bloom. The plants will adjust to varying temperatures without too much trouble. Potting should be done every year in medium-grade fir bark with the exception of *Brassavola digbyana*. This species resents root disturbance and the plant I have has not been repotted in four years. Instead I dig out the decayed compost and, with a blunt edged wood stick, add and push new bark in and around the root ball.

As with Cattleyas, allow the compost to dry out thoroughly between waterings. After flowering a short rest is necessary. During the dull season, waterings can be diminished somewhat.

I have found that cooler temperatures (52 to 58 degrees F. at night) will sometimes help initiate bud formation in *Brassavola digbyana* and *B. glauca*.

The genus responds well to summering out-of-doors and because of tough cactuslike foliage can tolerate direct sunshine.

BRASSIA

The *Brassias*, often called Spider Orchids, are epiphytes native to Southern Florida and Mexico with a few from Brazil and Peru. They are large evergreen plants with fantastic flowers, remarkable in that the sepals and petals are greatly elongated. *Brassia caudata, B. gireoudiana,* and *B. maculata—* are of easy culture and very handsome plants in flower.

These orchids have plump pseudobulbs about 2 to 6 inches long and somewhat leathery, dark green foliage 12 to 14 inches tall. The erect, or sometimes drooping, flower spikes

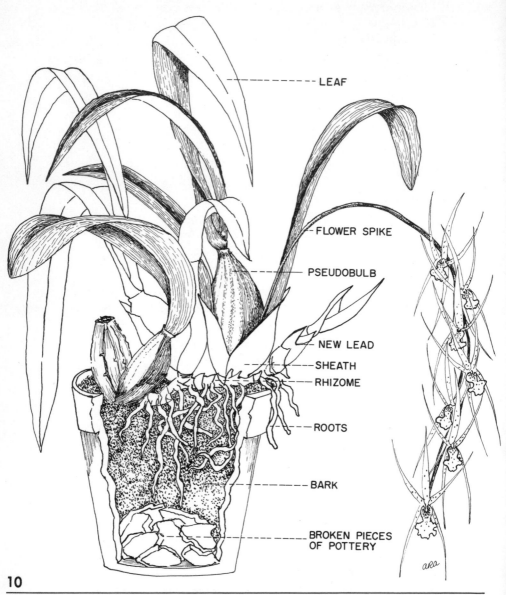

LEAF

FLOWER SPIKE

PSEUDOBULB

NEW LEAD

SHEATH

RHIZOME

ROOTS

BARK

BROKEN PIECES
OF POTTERY

10

BRASSIA MACULATA

produce numerous evenly-spaced flowers that appear in spring or summer lasting two or three weeks on the plant. The exotic fragrances are dividends of these fine plants.

B. maculata produces six to twelve flowers with sepals about 4 inches long, petals slightly shorter and greenish yellow spotted with brown, a white lip spreading and marked with brown or purple. This is a good Brassia to start with.

B. caudata makes a somewhat smaller plant with light green flowers, sometimes tinted yellow and spotted with dark brown on the lip.

B. gireoudiana with flower scapes sometimes reaching to 24 inches has several yellow or greenish yellow flowers with a few blotches of dark brown. The most fragrant of the group and a showpiece this species blooms irregularly. One year, my plant produced its flowers in September, the following year in June.

Brassias thrive in sun and a warm temperature. They resent root disturbance so I repot them only when necessary, usually every third year in large-grade fir bark in 8- to 10-inch clay pots. The plants are impatient of too much compost around the pseudobulbs and have a natural tendency to raise themselves out of the pot. This idiosyncrasy affords the grower an easy method of checking for healthy root tips.

The genus requires copious watering in active growth; fertilizing is also an aid at this time. At the end of summer to discourage foliage growth and help initiate flower spikes, I dry plants out slightly. These epiphytes benefit greatly from additional humidity but direct misting of the plants will produce bulb rot and should be avoided. Just mist the area. During the winter, watering can be decreased but do not allow the pseudobulbs to get dry enough to shrivel.

Although Brassias are easily brought into flower by most hobbyists, I had some trouble coaxing them into bloom. I now realize a night temperature of 52 to 58 degree F. in winter is too cold for them. I try to keep it around 56 to 62 degrees.

A summer outdoors will insure plump healthy bulbs on

these plants, and although the Brassia inflorescence lasts well on the plant, when cut and placed in water, they fade fast. These big plants deserve a place in every collection.

BULBOPHYLLUM

Bulbophyllum is a vast family of over 2,000 species distributed through Borneo, India, Burma, Malaya, Java, Madagascar, and Siam. There are also a great many native to New Guinea. They are unusual plants, many of dwarf stature, and like their cousins, the Cirrhopetalums, they produce flowers more curious than beautiful and in every color imaginable. Blossoms vary from the minute, hardly visible without a magnifying glass, to moderate 4-inch sizes. Though not generally difficult to grow, the Bulbophyllums are somewhat temperamental as to temperature and humidity. I have grown *Bulbophyllum barbigerum, B. careyanum, B. lemniscatoides, B. lobbii, B. macranthum, B. virescens*, and *B. ericssonii*. These do not flower for me as well as the Cirrhopetalums but mine are only second-year plants and sometimes these dwarf-types are slow to adjust to a new environment.

Most of the species have elongated rhizomes with 1-inch pseudobulbs terminating in one or two fleshy leaves, 2 to 6 inches long. Bloom is variable, and scapes are produced from, or near, the base of the bulbs. Some species carry dense racemes of umbrella form; others, solitary blossoms on tall stems. In some species, flowers have an unpleasant odor.

B. barbigerum has narrow greenish-brown sepals and petals; the yellow lip is long with two dark purple beards and a long purple brush of minute threads at the top. The slightest breath of air puts these threads in motion, giving the plant a lively appearance that delights children.

B. careyanum, although decorative with small reddish brown flowers, has an offensive odor.

B. lemniscatoides is a remarkable plant but difficult to lo-

11

BULBOPHYLLUM LOBBII (above)
CIRRHOPETALUM CUMINGII (below)

cate. The flower spike is drooping with many tiny dark purple flowers decked with white hairs and carrying white, rose-spotted, ribbonlike appendages.

B. lobbii grows larger than most of the other species and produces a different kind of inflorescence. The 12-inch plants carry an erect spike with a beautiful solitary 4-inch flower, copper-colored and sweet scented. A very handsome species, this requires a cool temperature of 52 to 58 degrees F. at night in winter.

B. macranthum has star-shaped flowers about 2 inches across. They are red, splashed with yellow. This is a good showy species to start with and easy to grow. It has blossomed twice for me since I bought it two years ago.

B. virescens produces a large flower head with six to ten greenish-yellow blossoms in an umbrella design. *B. ericssonii* is similar.

Bulbophyllums need filtered sunlight and more heat and humidity than the Cirrhopetalums. I suggest 62 to 68 degrees F. at night in winter and 72 to 80 degrees during the day with 70 percent humidity. Most of my Bulbophyllums grow on slabs of tree fern. They do not seem to do well in pots.

My plants are watered heavily when they are in active growth. As the pseudobulbs mature, usually in summer, I give them a rest of two to three weeks without any water. During the winter, I also decrease the amount somewhat.

Because most Bulbophyllums and Cirrhopetalums are of similar growth, they are sometimes incorrectly listed or sold without a species name. This is no disadvantage for usually these unidentified plants are cheaper, and sometimes you acquire a rare species. I consider species in either genus well worth the time and effort often required to get bloom.

CALANTHE

Calanthe is a large genus of mostly terrestrial orchids widely distributed through Asia, China, New Guinea, Madagascar, and the Fiji Islands with a few from the West Indies and Central America. This handsome genus is divided into two sections: the large-bulb deciduous types—*Calanthe vestita, C. rosea,* and *C. labrosa,* all of which I have grown; and the pseudobulbless evergreen types—*Calanthe biloba, C. masuca,* and *C. veratrifolia,* of which I have grown only *C. masuca.*

The deciduous species have elongated pseudobulbs of 8 to 12 inches bearing three or four broad paper-thin leaves 20 inches tall. When the leaves shed, the flower spike, erect or sometimes arching, is produced from the base of the bulbs and carries many small white or pink flowers during the Christmas season. They last five to seven weeks.

C. vestita and its varieties are the species most commonly grown. The flowers are 1 to 2 inches across, usually white or in shades of pink with variable color blotches at the base of the scalloped lip.

C. rosea produces small pale pink, almost white flowers.

C. labrosa has small rose-purple flowers, the lip dotted with purple.

Deciduous Calanthes require filtered sunlight when growth starts and full sun once leaves have expanded. Pot these terrestrials in March, or at signs of new growth, in a compost of loam, leaf mold, and sphagnum.

Water this group carefully until foliage expands. Then increase waterings and keep plants evenly moist through the summer. Towards fall when foliage sheds, reduce waterings considerably to encourage flower spikes. Once apparent (2 to 3 inches long) apply moisture until buds are plump, *taking care not to wet the spike.* When the first flowers open, stop watering entirely. After flowering is over, I cut the spike off, knock the plant from the pot and place the bulbs in a brown-paper sack and store at 60 degrees F. When potting the following spring, I separate the bulbs. Because of the folded nature of Calanthe leaves, I never mist them.

I keep six pots of these Christmas-blooming orchids. For table decoration or as cut flowers placed in water in a small vase they are hard to beat.

IN ACTIVE GROWTH

/IN FLOWER

12

DECIDUOUS CALANTHE VESTITA

Even out of bloom, evergreen Calanthes make handsome house plants resembling Chinese evergreens. The tall folded leaves are dark green and grow in a compact bunch. The inflorescence, borne on a stout spike sometimes 30 inches tall, is clustered. The individual purple or rose-colored flowers, smaller than those of the deciduous group, appear through the summer.

C. masuca has six to twelve flowers 2 inches across, blue-violet, the lip purple. A very free-flowering species.

C. biloba is slightly different in structure and has 6- to 8-inch stemlike growths that carry 8- to 12-inch leaves. The small flowers, 1 inch across, are purplish, tinted yellow.

C. veratrifolia has several 1-inch white flowers usually with a yellow splotch in the center of the lip. There are many varieties of this species and the colors differ somewhat.

Evergreen Calanthes need filtered sunlight. Although they are not particular about temperature, warm and humid growing conditions suit them best. Potting should be done yearly in a terrestrial compost or in fir bark with shredded tree fern.

During growth, even moisture is necessary but do not fertilize; I find this burns the foliage. When new growth is completed, afford a four-week dry rest and move to a cooler place (55 to 60 degrees F. at night). Resume watering but sparingly through the dull months.

CATASETUM

Catasetum is a large genus of epiphytic orchids confined mainly to Central America, and the flowers are possibly the most remarkable in the orchid world. The intricate structure is fascinating and because the plants carry both male and female forms that vary in size and color, great confusion has resulted in the classification of the genus. The flowers are greenish or white or yellow or brown and often splotched or

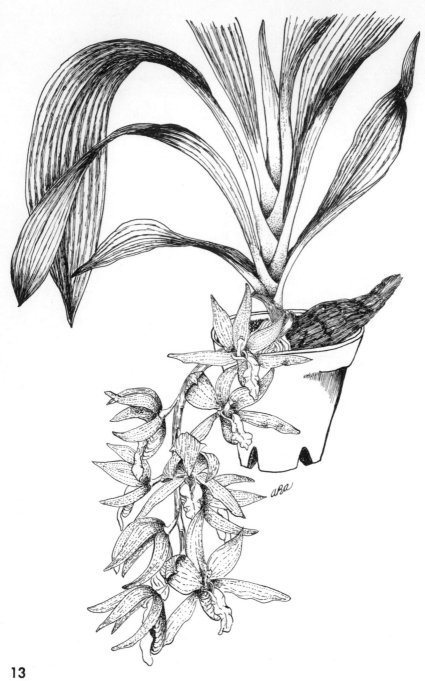

13

barred. Although not commonly seen, *Catasetum pileatum*, *C. russellianum*, and *C. scurra* were secured inexpensively, and recently I also purchased a fine plant of *C. viridiflavum*.

Plants have short stout almost pointed pseudobulbs 6 to 12 inches tall with large light green deciduous or semideciduous leaves. Flower scapes are erect or sometimes pendant and are produced from the base of the mature pseudobulb or from the new growth. They carry many flowers during spring or summer, usually scented and lasting well on the plant.

C. pileatum has large white flowers with an oyster shell-like lip. A very handsome but hard to find plant.

C. russellianum produces flowers 2 inches across, pale green, veined with dark green lines. The plant is very free flowering and always distinguished by a strong scent of roses.

C. scurra is a small-growing species never more than 10 inches tall and has white flowers about an inch across.

Catasetums thrive in a sunny position at the window but only after the leaves have fallen. Because the fleshy pseudobulbs are intolerant of overwatering, the plants will usually come to you on slabs of cork bark or tree fern so that you do not have to repot for three or four years. Pot culture is also acceptable and in this case repotting should be done every second year. A warm moist atmosphere is essential for healthy growth.

Rest these epiphytes without water in October or after the growing season. Once flower spikes appear, take great care not to wet them, as they rot easily. Only after the spike is well under way should watering be resumed, and then sparingly. During the dull months, water only occasionally.

Catasetums do well with a summer outdoors where I water them daily through the short growing season and where natural air currents dry them quickly.

From about November until March this genus is inactive and will require very little care. A most worthwhile group of plants for those seeking the unusual.

CATTLEYA

The genus *Cattleya* with its thousands of hybrids is certainly the best known of all orchids. Mainly epiphytes, about seventy species are widely distributed from Mexico to Brazil and these plants, although not so large or showy as the hybrids, are still very desirable, producing richly colored flowers. The dwarf species of the genus, are for the most part of easy culture, and ideal plants since a window shelf can accommodate six or eight of them. *Cattleya aclandiae, C. citrina, C. dolosa, C. forbesii, C. nobilior, C. skinneri* which I have grown and *C. luteola, C. o'brieniana,* and *C. schilleriana* are a few of the many available.

When full grown these epiphytes are about 12 inches tall with pseudobulbs 2 to 4 inches long and usually one or two stiff fleshy leaves. The majority of the plants produce flower scapes from the apex of the last-made pseudobulb and while in bud are protected by a tight sheath. Mainly summer flowering, a great many are sweet scented and the inflorescence remains in good condition for two to four weeks.

C. aclandiae for me produces one or two flowers, 4 inches across, olive-green and blotched with brown-purple, the lip magenta with darker purple. I grow this plant on a slab of tree fern in preference to pot culture. It seems the better method.

C. citrina is one of the few of the genus that blooms in pendant fashion. The cup-shaped flowers, 2 inches across, are bright yellow and very pretty. Since the plant hangs down, I grow it on a block of wood or slab of fern.

C. dolosa has magenta-colored flowers with a yellow disc in the lip and is winter flowering.

C. forbesii makes a somewhat larger plant and carries two to five flowers, $3\frac{1}{2}$ inches across, greenish yellow, the lip yellow streaked with red on the inside.

14

CATTLEYA FORBESII

C. nobilior has delicate rose-colored flowers, the inflorescence borne on a separate leafless stem. A most unusual species.

C. luteola is a small plant 6 inches tall with a 2-inch pale yellow flower with a white lip, sides streaked with purple.

C. o'brieniana bears one to three large rose-colored flowers, front part of lip darker.

C. schilleriana produces large dark rose-brown flowers 4 inches across with a dark rose lip edged with pink. This blooms in late summer. When the pseudobulbs mature, give five- to seven-week bone-dry rest.

C. skinneri grows to about 30 inches and produces two to eight rose-purple flowers about 3 inches across.

During the summer, I grow Cattleyas at a west window where they receive three to five hours of afternoon sun. In winter, the plants are moved to a south or east window. Potting in fir bark or osmunda every year after flowering or before new growth appears insures healthy plants. Pot tight and hard.

Allow Cattleyas to dry out thoroughly between watering, even when they are in active growth. After the flowers fade, give a complete rest of five to seven weeks without water but with an occasional misting.

Temperate house conditions will suit this genus, but during the dull resting months a cooler temperature is better (58 to 62 degrees F. at night in winter).

These plants benefit greatly from a summer outdoors on a porch or suspended from tree branches by pot hangers.

Once in flower, Cattleyas can be moved anywhere in the house for decoration and, as small lapel flowers, they are most attractive, too.

CHYSIS

Chysis is a small genus of strange and very showy epiphytic orchids from Mexico, Central America, and northern

South America. There are about six species available and all are worth growing since the flowers are of different colors. The varieties, *Chysis aurea, C. bractescens,* and *C. laevis* are most commonly seen.

The genus is a curiosity because of an unusual manner of growth; the large cigar-shaped pseudobulbs are 10 to 12 inches long and generally hang down over the rim of the pot. Since the plants are deciduous or semideciduous, these long bulbs are bare for most of the year. The thin plicated leaves grow about 12 to 15 inches high and appear in early spring simultaneously with the flowers. The leaves sometimes grow in pendant fashion. Chysis varieties bloom in spring or early summer, the blossoms lasting two to three weeks on the plant.

C. aurea produces flowers about 3 inches across, tawny yellow often marked with crimson, lip fleshy, mostly crimson.

C. bractescens has large thick flowers on short, slightly arched racemes that push out from the new growth. The inflorescence is cup-shaped and clustered. Generally, my plants have three or five showy flowers about 4 inches across, white with yellow centers, the texture like that of gardenias and with a powerful spicy scent.

C. laevis is perhaps the handsomest of the genus with yellow-orange flowers $2\frac{1}{2}$ inches across, fringed, and marked with red. Though smaller, the flowers seemed to me truly eye-catching in my window.

These epiphytes do well with two to three hours of strong sun a day. In active growth, they require liberal watering and fertilizing. After bulbs are matured, keep plants dry; generally they will shed leaves. At this time I find it best to move the plants to lower temperatures (55 to 58 degrees F. at night). When new growth appears, I move them back to a slightly warmer place and resume watering.

Chyses should be repotted every third year but since they have a great aversion to any root disturbance, I try to avoid it and instead dig out the decayed compost with a blunt-

15

CHYSIS BRACTESCENS

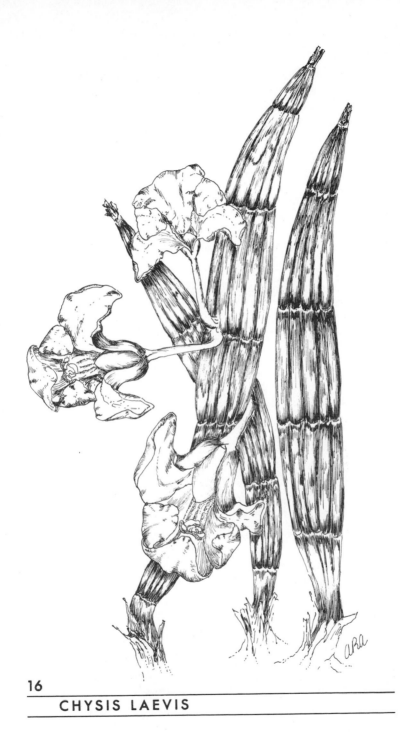

16

CHYSIS LAEVIS

edged stick and then fill in and push down fresh bark or osmunda as best as I can. Although some growers recommend growing this genus in slanted baskets so the pseudobulbs can hang vertically, I grow mine in regular slotted clay pots and have even staked *C. laevis* without damage to the plant.

The thin foliage of Chysis is susceptible to red spider so undersides of leaves should be checked periodically. If there is an infestation, I wash the leaves with a soft brush dipped in soap and water or in a mild solution of nicotine sulphate (Black Leaf 40).

CIRRHOPETALUM

Cirrhopetalum is a genus of about fifty species widely distributed through India, China, and Australia and so closely related to *Bulbophyllum* that the two genera are often confused. The small plants produce blooms of remarkable construction, each tiny flower having a place in the perfect pattern of a circle or arc. Many are put into motion by the slightest current of air and some people think them carnivorous, but they are not. The bright flowers last only about a week. I have been successful with *Cirrhopetalum cumingii, C. longissimum, C. ornatissimum,* and *C. mastersianum.* These small orchids are easy to grow and take up little space. One or two species are delightful in any collection.

Most of the species are characterized by a creeping rhizome. The pseudobulb is about an inch long, usually four-angled and tipped with a thick, solitary leaf, 3 to 8 inches long. The wiry flower spike is leafless and produced from the side of the pseudobulb. The season is variable but the majority bloom in summer.

C. cumingii (Figure 11, page 45) is a masterpiece of tiny, vivid, ruby-red flowers arranged in a half circle. This is a good species to start with and a most interesting plant.

C. mastersianum has slightly larger flowers, tawny orange, in umbrella form, and carried on an arching spike. This one is a beauty sometimes producing two or three flower stalks from one pseudobulb.

C. ornatissimum, although not as pretty as others in the family, is interesting. The flowers are pale purple-brown about 3 inches long; sepals and petals are tufted with hairs and the lip is red-purple. It has a rather unpleasant odor.

C. longissimum produces flowers remarkable for the length of the side sepals which are sometimes 12 inches long. They are ice-cream pink or buff with purple lines running to a purple spot. This flowers in winter for me and is spectacular.

Cirrhopetalums thrive under my home conditions where temperatures range from 58 to 62 degrees F. at night in winter and 62 to 76 degrees F. during the day. I recommend growing these orchids on tree-fern slab. Wrap the root ball in damp osmunda and wire it to the slab. The few plants of this genus that I tried to grow in pots did not do well, probably because they are so intolerant of a sour growing mixture.

A west window with three to four hours of afternoon sunlight will suit the Cirrhopetalums. At a south exposure, they need some shading, placed perhaps back of larger orchids. From March to September my plants are watered daily, that is, water is poured over the tree slab and runs off into a clay saucer. Propped against window sill or post, the lowest inch or two of the slab can safely rest in water. In fact, this may be my key to successful growing for the slab absorbs the water during the day, keeping the plants evenly moist most of the time. In winter, watering is decreased somewhat but I still do not allow these orchids to become bone dry.

You will find that Cirrhopetalums make fine house plants. Although they are not plentiful, you will be able to locate the species mentioned here from sources listed at the end of this book.

COELOGYNE

Coelogyne is a genus of more than 150 species widely distributed throughout India, Malaya, New Guinea, and southern China. Mostly epiphytic, these evergreen plants are handsome even out of flower and because a great number are forest dwellers that prefer dappled sunlight, they are ideal plants for window culture. The flowers are mainly brown or yellow or white or green and appear in winter or spring. The pendant-type Coelogynes are especially beautiful with twenty to thirty flowers to a stem. I have grown *Coelogyne cristata, C. flaccida, C. fuscescens, C. gardneriana, C. massangeana, C. meyeriana, C. ochracea, C. pandurata,* and *C. speciosa alba,* which are only a few of this vast and amenable family.

Plants differ in growth habit but usually have pear-shaped or ovoid pseudobulbs bearing one or two leaves. The flower scapes are erect or decidedly pendulous and generally arise from the center of new growth. The long-lasting flowers also vary considerably in size and are usually scented.

C. cristata, the most common species, produces drooping racemes of white flowers with a yellow stained lip.

C. flaccida is a small plant, about 14 inches tall, with creamy white flowers about an inch across, the throat and side lobes lined purple-brown.

C. fuscescens, a plant with creeping rhizomes, has small greenish flowers suffused brownish red, the lip marked cinnamon color. This one can be trained to grow up a fernwood pole.

C. gardneriana is a compact plant that bears white flowers with a yellow lip, a mark of brown at the base. This species dislikes strong sun and is a good plant for those orphan north windows.

C. meyeriana is a rambling variety with creeping rhizomes.

COELOGYNE MASSANGEANA

18

COELOGYNE SPECIOSA ALBA

It is best grown in an open orchid basket. The inflorescence is large and greenish, the lip marked black.

C. massangeana, a large variety sometimes 2 feet tall, produces long pendant stems of evenly-spaced ochre-brown flowers, the lip marked with maroon. A robust species, this soon becomes pot bound. It blooms freely, sometimes twice a year.

C. ochracea brings spring to any window with masses of very fragrant small white flowers bordered with orange. A real charmer, it needs some sun, so a south or west exposure would be best.

C. pandurata, sometimes called the black orchid, is a big plant with handsome apple-green flowers 4 inches across, the lip marked with broad black veins ending in a triangular black splotch. This shy-blooming species needs heat to about 78 degrees and night temperatures should never fall below 60 degrees. A 50 to 70 percent humidity is essential too.

C. speciosa alba, a small plant, rarely growing to more than 12 inches, bears 5-inch flowers, beige-colored, extremely delicate in appearance and very decorative. This is a free-flowering species that may bloom at any time of year. Although it produces only one flower at a time, there are usually two or three flowers to a spike (one opening as another fades). My plant blossomed in late fall and again the following spring. A desirable and beautiful orchid, well worth a search, for it is not easy to find.

Grow Coelogynes in dappled sunlight with as much humidity as possible. Although they are notoriously intolerant of root disturbance, I generally repot them about every eighteen months, with the exception of *C. massangeana* which remains pot bound. The species *C. meyeriana* and *C. pandurata* have creeping rhizomes and require long baskets. Tight, hard potting in osmunda or fir bark mixed with sphagnum insures good health.

In active growth, these epiphytes require a great deal of watering, but after the flowers fade, a complete rest of five to seven weeks is necessary. An exception to this is *C. pandurata*, which should be kept moist all through the year.

Don't let water lodge in the new growth of plants in this genus, for in most cases the immature inflorescence is inside and this will rot if kept wet.

Coelogynes are my favorite orchids for they are dependable plants for the home and produce flowers without special attention.

CYCNOCHES

Commonly known as the Swan Orchid, *Cycnoches* is a small genus of eleven species native to Mexico and Brazil. *Cynoches chlorochilon*, often sold as *C. ventricosum*, since the plants are similar, is the most widely grown. The variety *C. egertonianum* is different but difficult to locate. Allied to *Catasetum* and *Mormodes*, Cycnoches plants produce curious large flowers of a greenish color in late summer or early fall.

These deciduous plants have cylindrical elongated pseudobulbs 4 to 8 inches long with large folded leaves. The flower scapes, arching or pendant, arise from the top of the bulbs between the leaf axils and carry a variable number of usually scented flowers that last three to five weeks on the plant.

C. chlorochilon has the largest flower of the genus, measuring 7 inches across. They are yellow-green, almost chartreuse, with a creamy white lip blotched with dark green. Because of the waxy texture of the inflorescence, it appears artificial but the heavy morning fragrance, clean and spicy, is delightfully real. Free flowering and most adaptable to window culture, this species in most cases retains foliage till after flowering.

C. egertonianum has flowers 2 inches across, greenish tan with a pure white or green lip.

Cycnoches requires a warm temperature, good humidity,

CYCNOCHES CHLOROCHILON

and filtered sun rather than direct sunshine. *Repot every year* in 5- or 6-inch clay pots using medium-grade fir bark and strive for perfect drainage. This is essential.

During active growth, keep these epiphytes just evenly moist; overwatering rots the pseudobulbs. Upon completion of growth, plants need a two- to four-week rest. Resume watering when the flower spike appears. In the winter months, very little water is necessary.

CYPRIPEDIUM

Cypripedium, botanically called Paphiopedilum, is a genus of fifty species of Asiatic origin. *Phragmipedium* represents the South American section of the family and is sometimes mistakenly called *Selenipedium*, an entirely different genus and rarely seen. Cypripedium hybrids are popular as cut flowers being large, showy, and long-lasting. The blooms are weirdly fascinating and in lurid color combinations. The waxy inflorescence often seems more artificial than real. The species are also popular with collectors for they too are handsome and adapt well to window-sill culture. The plants are mainly terrestrial. The family is complex with some species requiring warm, and others, cool conditions. I highly recommend *Cypripedium bellatulum, C. concolor, C. insigne,* and *C. niveum,* all of which have bloomed regularly for me.

The genus is without pseudobulbs and has dark green or mottled strap foliage in a handsome fan formation attached to a fleshy rhizome. The flower spike comes from the center of the leaves and carries one or several flowers that last five to seven weeks on the plant.

C. bellatulum has leaves 10 inches long and cup-shaped flowers with broad petals, white or pale yellow, and marked with purple spots.

C. concolor is popular and easy to grow. It is a small plant

CYPRIPEDIUM INSIGNE

2   White-flowered *Cypripedium niveum* for summer

with leaves about 6 inches long and yellow-speckled flowers with crimson dots.

C. insigne grows somewhat larger and has brown-veined apple-green flowers of shiny waxy texture. Many varieties are available in a wide range of color.

C. niveum with 10-inch leaves bears small, satiny, white flowers speckled purple. A very charming plant and a good "Cyp" to start with.

Cypripediums do best at a semishaded window where there is diffused light. The species I have grown accommodate to home temperatures of about 58 degrees at night in winter. Because the plants are without pseudobulbs, even moisture is necessary all year, but water should never remain in the crowns of the plants or rot may result. Repotting in 4- to 5-inch pots is done annually after flowering. My tertrial compost is composed of osmunda mixed with sphagnum moss and a little leaf mold; it suits most of the Cyps. This genus is slightly temperamental about repotting, so be gentle and take care not to injure any of the roots.

Temperature requirements vary from cool to warm depending upon the individual species. *Cypripedium callosum* and *C. villosum* should be grown at a cool 50 to 55 degrees at night in winter. *C. fairrieanum* and *C. curtisii* needs 55 to 62 degrees F., *C. barbatum* and *C. rothschildianum* 62 to 72 degrees F. Keep these three heat requirements in mind when you select your plants.

DENDROBIUM

Dendrobium is among the largest of all orchid genera with more than 1,500 species widely distributed through the world. Many are from India, Burma, and Ceylon, others from parts of China and Japan, and a great number are native to Australia and the Philippines. The species vary greatly in shape and habit but all produce beautiful flowers. They can be divided into five groups: those with 1) pronounced pseudobulbs; 2) evergreen cane-type pseudobulbs; 3) deciduous cane-type pseudobulbs; 4) evergreen cane-type Phalaenopsis hybrids; and 5) black-haired short-stemmed plants.

I have grown *Dendrobium chrysotoxum* and *D. aggregatum* of the first group; these are of easy culture and highly recommended for the beginner. The plants need about four hours of sun a day and abundant watering until growth is mature. Then to encourage flower spikes a rest period of three to four weeks without water is in order. After flowering, allow a complete rest of five to seven weeks without water. Repot every second year in 4- or 5-inch pots.

D. chrysotoxum grows 20 inches high and produces drooping apical spikes of many 2-inch golden-yellow flowers in spring. It often blooms from old as well as new bulbs.

D. aggregatum, a dwarf plant about 10 inches high produces from the sides of the pseudobulbs pendant spikes covered with small, scented, vivid yellow flowers. This species

21

DENDROBIUM AGGREGATUM

has flowered for me regularly for the last five years, always in March.

The evergreen cane-type plants include *D. densiflorum, D. thyrsiflorum,* and *D. dalhousieanum;* there are others available but because they are usually big plants, sometimes over 6 feet tall, I have only grown these three. The apical leaves are broad and fleshy. Flowers are produced in pendant trusses from the nodes at the top of the canes; they are set close together and perfectly arranged like a bunch of grapes, unbelievably pretty. Dappled sunlight is needed for these plants and even moisture throughout the year except just after flowering, when water can be somewhat reduced for about a month.

Repot these Dendrobiums every second year in fir bark in 4- or 5-inch pots. Home temperatures of 58 to 64 degrees at night in winter are adequate with 72 to 80 degrees during the day. If you have trouble flowering the "Dendrobes" try resting them for about three weeks after growth has matured, and move them then closer to the window where the 5- to 6-degree drop may induce bud formation in winter. They produce their beautiful flowers in spring or early summer.

D. dalhousieanum has flowers 5 inches across; they are tawny yellow, almost beige, and faintly shaded crimson.

D. thyrsiflorum has bunches of striking crystal-white flowers with an orange lip. *This is a magnificent species and should be in every home collection.*

D. densiflorum is similar to others in the group but with flowers of somewhat deeper yellow.

The deciduous cane-type Dendrobiums, commonly called the "nobile" section, produce flowers in two's and three's from the nodes along the top of the bare canes. There are several species. The plants I have been successful with are *Dendrobium fimbriatum, D. nobile, D. pierardii, D. wardianum,* and *D. superbum.* Flowers are large and delicate, in shades of pink, lavender, and orange; a great many of them scented. In growth through the summer, these fine orchids need moisture and warmth, but when foliage has fully expanded with a solitary leaf instead of pairs of leaves, stop watering. At this time, usually October, I move my plants to an unheated pantry that has a south window where the temperature is 48 to 55 degrees at night. Through the winter while the leaves fall, they receive *no water*. When buds start to show in swellings along the nodes, I move the plants back to their regular trays at a west window where the temperature is 58 to 64 degrees at night, and I resume waterings as buds increase in size. These are repotted every second year in 4- or 5-inch pots.

D. fimbriatum sheds its foliage every second year. It's a pretty little plant that bears brilliant orange flowers. A good one to try.

D. nobile, the most popular one, has flowers of white tipped rose-purple with a dark crimson blotch in the throat. There are many wonderful hybrids of this species and color varies.

D. pierardii produces 2-inch paper-thin flowers. They are blush-white or pink and veined rose-purple. A very dependable plant.

D. wardianum with 2-foot stems has white flowers tipped purple with a yellow-stained lip. This plant is a shy bloomer, flowering only twice in five years for me.

D. superbum produces myriads of handsome large lilac-colored flowers from bare silver-hued canes. This species is extremely handsome and requires vertical growing space for canes sometimes 5 to 6 feet long.

The evergreen cane-type *D. phalaenopsis* grow to about 2 feet and produce flowers on short stems from the top of the canes. *D. veratrifolium*, known as the "antelope orchid," is in this group but a rare species to find. Temperatures of 72 to 80 degrees with at least four hours of sun a day and abundant moisture are necessary for good flower production. The temperature should never drop below 70 degrees at night in winter. Although I have grown most Dendrobiums successfully, this group has continually fooled me. The two plants

3 Pale rose, pendent-flowering *Dendrobium pierardii* for spring

I have, flower irregularly but where a warm climate prevails the year round, I have seen them in magnificent form.

D. *phalaenopsis* produces many flowers about 3 inches across, deep rose shaded magenta. There are many hybrids so colors vary considerably.

D. *veratrifolium* produces lovely fragrant flowers, about 3 inches across.

Although the inflorescence of the other groups mentioned here last well on the plant, three to four weeks, the black-haired short-stemmed Formosum or Dearei Dendrobiums are amazing for flower durability. Blossoms sometimes remain perfect for cight to eleven weeks. D. *dearei*, D. *formosum*, and D. *jamesianum* are a few of this group. Characterized by black-haired silvery stems, plants produce white flowers in apical clusters, the lip usually spotted yellow or red. I successfully flowered D. *jamesianum*, sometimes called D. *in-*

fundibulum var. *jamesianum* at a west window with temperatures of 54 to 62 at night in winter. I kept it moist most of the year except after flowering when it was dried out for three weeks and then reported. I have not tried any others in the group as they are difficult to obtain. Most of the species flower late in summer.

Any of this genus can be summered out-of-doors in direct sun once growth is well under way. Mealy bugs may appear on leaves of the deciduous group so inspect plants regularly.

EPIDENDRUM

Epidendrum is one of the larger orchid genera with about 1,000 species distributed mainly through Central America, Mexico, Brazil, and tropical America. These terrestrial or epiphytic plants are variable in form. Some have globose or hard egg-shaped pseudobulbs, some have stemlike pseudobulbs, others are without pseudobulbs and have flexible or reedlike stems. Flowers come in every color imaginable and many species bloom throughout the year.

I have grown *Epidendrum atropurpureum, E. aromaticum,* and *E. vitellinum* of the hard-bulb group. The pseudobulb is tipped with two leaves and the arching spike comes from the top of the bulb and bears many flowers that last three to five weeks on the plant. These species require direct sun and tight hard potting in osmunda or fir bark. Plenty of water is necessary while plants are in active growth and until flowering. Then a pronounced rest of three to five weeks is needed with very little water. In dull months, waterings can also be decreased somewhat.

E. aromaticum, about 12 inches tall, produces greenish-white flowers powerfully but sweetly scented; *E. atropurpureum,* similar in habit, has brown-and-pink flowers with a red-striped lip. Both species bloom in early spring and are

EPIDENDRUM ATROPURPUREUM

amenable to home temperatures of 58 to 64 degrees at night in winter and 70 to 78 degrees during the day.

E. vitellinum is a dwarf species about 8 inches tall with brilliant small red flowers. This is a charming window plant that should be placed close to the glass for it likes coolness, about 54 to 60 degrees at night.

Epidendrum stamfordianum, and *E. prismatocarpum* represent the stemlike pseudobulb species similar in habit to *Cattleya.* They make large plants that grow slowly. I have had room in my collection only for *E. stamfordianum.* The plants need filtered sunshine and are better potted slightly loose in osmunda or fir bark mixed with sphagnum. Even moisture is needed throughout the year with perhaps a slight rest for a few weeks after flowering. They are slow to come back with new growth so do not try to force them. Average home temperatures around 70 degrees suit these species.

E. stamfordianum produces erect scapes of brilliant yellow flowers spotted red. The inflorescence is bunched at the top of the stem, lasts well, and is delightfully fragrant. This species produces its flower spike from near the base of the pseudobulb. I find it does best with a complete rest of five to seven weeks (no water) after flowering.

E. prismatocarpum has bright yellow flowers blotched vivid purple. I have not tried this showy plant but have seen it in bloom in other collections and it is a real eye-catcher.

The reed-stem Epidendrums without pseudobulbs are known for constant blossoming. I have had a plant of *E. o'brienianum* in flower for over a year; *E. elegans* and *E. nocturnum* are also worthwhile. These require plenty of water all year and a few hours of south or west sun. Repotting is necessary every year. Average home temperatures suit them.

E. o'brienianum has 1-inch flowers clustered at the top. As the lowest flowers fade, new ones appear at the top. There are many varieties and colors range from pink to lavender to brick red. In climates mild the year-round, this plant will do well outside in a garden, in a standard terrestrial compost.

23

EPIDENDRUM STAMFORDIANUM

E. elegans produces flowers about 2 inches across. They are dark rose with a white lip streaked crimson.

E. nocturnum has 4-inch greenish-white flowers especially fragrant at night. It likes slightly cool conditions.

For a start in this group try *E. o'brienianum;* it is available and inexpensive. The other two species may be difficult to locate.

GONGORA

Gongora, a genus of about thirty species, once very popular, is seldom seen in cultivation now. Yet the species are easy to grow and very floriferous. Sometimes a small plant in a 5-inch pot will produce seven or eight spikes of pendant flowers, as many as thirty on a scape; not really pretty but decorative. Epiphytes from Mexico, Central America, and Brazil they are represented by the species *Gongora armeniaca* and *G. galeata,* both of which have flowered regularly for me.

Resembling Stanhopeas, the plants are more compact with conical, ribbed pseudobulbs and broad evergreen leaves. The drooping scapes, sometimes 3 feet long, are produced from the base of the pseudobulbs and bear many close-set, medium-size flowers contorted in form with the petals folded back. Sweet-scented, the flowers appear in late summer for me.

G. armeniaca, sometimes called *Acropera armeniaca,* produces apricot flowers on a greenish-purple scape. The waxy lip is vivid yellow. A very showy plant and a good Gongora to try.

G. galeata, also known as *Acropera loddigesii,* has pale, tawny-yellow flowers with a brownish-red lip. Several varieties of different coloring are available.

A place with diffused sun is best for this genus and temperatures of 58 to 64 at night in winter, 72 to 80 degrees F. during the day. Good air circulation is necessary, and it is

24

GONGORA ARMENIACA

best to repot every second year. Large-grade fir bark seems to make the best compost.

When they are growing, keep these epiphytes evenly moist; my plants are watered daily in summer. A different culture has been recommended for this genus but after some trial and error, I have found that in the home, daily watering is best. In winter, when bulbs have matured, decrease moisture somewhat. For about three weeks in January, I give my plants a complete rest without any water.

Gongoras have the habit of pushing forth many flower stems. When there are four or five of these, I snip off one or two, for I have found that the plant cannot support so many scapes. These orchids, when in bud, have an aversion to drafts or fluctuating temperatures. Otherwise, they are rather easy to grow. Although still considered only for the collector, they certainly deserve more attention from hobbyists. They are readily available and not expensive.

HEXISEA

Not a large genus, *Hexisea* with about five species from Central America has a very charming plant in the family called *Hexisea bidentata*. This orchid is easily grown and dependable for the beginner.

Hexiseas are unusual in growth with thin pseudobulbs, one sprouting from another in a chain. Flowers are produced in clumps at the very end. The leaves are only 3 to 4 inches long and look like tufted blades of thin grass. If planted on a tree-fern slab, the plant will ramble all over and off the slab. Even a young specimen in a 3-inch pot will blossom.

H. bidentata bears clusters of bright-red flowers about an inch long in spring or summer.

The genus seems to do well under average conditions, being amenable to temperature variation. My plant flourishes at a south window and is watered daily in spring and summer,

about twice a week the rest of the year. A charming house
plant.

HUNTLEYA

Huntleya, a genus of perhaps three species, is native to
Costa Rica and Brazil. It is a spectacular family but the
species are still rare in cultivation. I bought my plant out of
flower. Although I expected a handsome orchid, I was, in-
deed, overwhelmed when it opened. Correctly called Huntleya, species in this genus are still sold as *Zygopetalum*. The
only available species is *Huntleya meleagris*, also offered as
H. burtii.

Even out of flower, Huntleyas are handsome plants. The
light green leaves, about 12 inches long, grow in a fan. They
are brittle so take care not to snap them off accidentally. The
short scapes are produced from leaf axils and bear but one
flower. The plant I have had two scapes, one from each side,
and the flowers lasted about two weeks on the plant.

H. meleagris produces a large flower, about 5 inches across,
star-shaped with a thick waxy texture like that of a bromeliad.
It is reddish brown suffused with yellow, the lip pure-white
marked with brown and purple; the crest is fringed.

Huntleyas are scarce because they do not often survive the
fumigation at ports of entry. Furthermore, they are sensitive
to temperature change and, although they require an evenly
moist compost, they are intolerant of too much water at the
roots. My plant, in large-grade fir bark mixed with sphagnum
moss, grows in broken sunlight at a temperature of about 58
degrees F. at night in winter. In summer, I keep the plant as
cool as possible, and at all times give it good air circulation.

LAELIA

Laelia is a genus closely allied to *Cattleya* with about seventy species from South America. The majority require a place at a south window in direct sun and even then these handsome plants may not bloom. I have grown and flowered *Laelia autumnalis, L. flava, L. pumila,* and recently have coaxed *L. superbiens* into spike. Such sun-loving epiphytes are a challenge but certainly worthwhile.

Generally, these orchids carry one or two fleshy evergreen leaves. The pseudobulbs vary in size and shape and the flower spike is produced from the top of the pseudobulb. Several of the species are dwarf plants that produce brilliant yellow or orange flowers at various times of year. Others make extremely large plants carrying spikes 6 feet long and crowded with spectacular bloom. These can be grown in the house if placed on inverted pots on the floor. Put them in front of a window or near French doors where they can receive ample sunshine.

L. autumnalis grows to about 12 inches and produces an inflorescence 4 inches across, rose or pinkish purple, the lip white with a yellow ridge.

L. flava is a 10-inch plant with clusters of charming canary-yellow flowers.

L. pumila, a 6-inch dwarf species, has pretty rose-purple flowers 2 inches across, large for the size of the plant. This is a good Laelia to start with.

L. superbiens is a giant, 3 to 4 feet tall, with flower scapes 4 to 6 feet long. I mention this species because it is perhaps one of the most beautiful orchids grown. Large clusters of ten to fifteen flowers are a brilliant rose streaked with crimson or purple. I have seen it in bloom at conservatories, where crowds of people gather round it.

The Laelia family grows under such varied conditions that

25

LAELIA PUMILA

it is impossible to be very definite about culture. The plants I flowered were given plenty of sun and abundant moisture until they blossomed. Then I moved them to my unheated pantry where temperatures range from 52 to 56 degrees F. at night in winter. After a four-week rest, I resumed watering but sparingly through the winter months. In early spring, they go back in the plant room and in summer, I grow Laelias outside on the back porch where they get the sun they need, about five hours a day.

About every two years, I repot big plants of this genus in large-grade fir bark; the small plants in small-grade bark.

LOCKHARTIA

Lockhartia, commonly called the Braided Orchid, is a genus of some twenty species native to Central America. The overlapping foliage is unusual, and the plants produce mainly yellow flowers. Even out of bloom, they are interesting. These epiphytes are easy to grow, the three most popular species being *Lockhartia oerstedii*, *L. acuta*, and *L. lunifera*. These are much alike so you probably won't want more than one species of this family.

Without pseudobulbs, Lockhartias usually have arching stems to 2½ feet and covered with small, bright-green leaves. The foliage is in a clump and flowers are produced on short scapes dangling from the upper part of the stems. They remind me of Christmas tree ornaments. Most species bloom through spring and summer. Select mature plants to get good flower production; they are inexpensive.

L. oerstedii has many solitary, yellow flowers spotted red.

L. acuta produces clusters of flowers with the same coloring.

L. lunifera has a slightly larger flower, about 1 inch long, also bright yellow and red.

This genus requires diffused light rather than direct sun. I

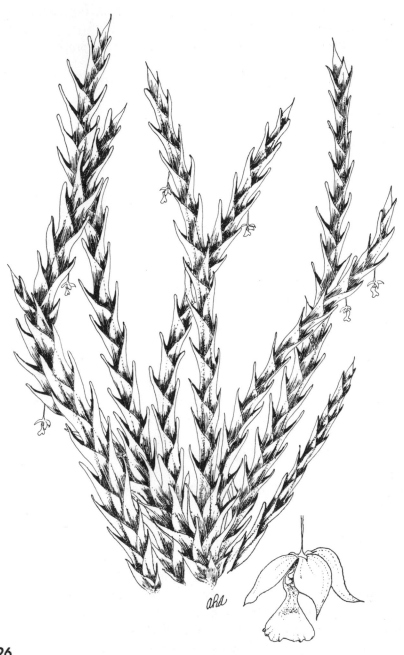

LOCKHARTIA OERSTEDII

repot my Lockhartia every second year in straight osmunda. Tight hard potting in small pots is best.

These plants should never be allowed to dry out completely but a stale compost must also be avoided. The best method seems to be to soak plants thoroughly once a week from April to September, and about every two weeks the rest of the year. These orchids will grow in cool or warm temperatures but about 62 degrees at night in winter will suit them best.

Although not showy, Lockhartias are little trouble and have a charm of their own.

LYCASTE

Mostly epiphytic, the *Lycaste,* a genus of about thirty species, includes handsome orchids from Mexico, Cuba, Peru, and Brazil, and these often respond better to window culture than greenhouse treatment. Plants are deciduous or semideciduous, and the long-lasting flowers vary greatly in size and color. Unlike other genera, the pseudobulbs of Lycaste produce several flower spikes, a most happy faculty for a plant can have as many as six to ten flowers. *Lycaste aromatica, L. deppei, L. skinneri,* and *L. gigantea* are a few members of this wonderful group. I have grown all but the last one.

The plants have fan-shaped clumps of leaves 2 to 3 feet tall. Flowers are usually carried on short erect scapes from the base of the last-made pseudobulb, often after the leaves have shed and along with the young growth. Although mainly winter flowering, it is not until early spring that my plants blossom.

L. aromatica is of dwarf growth, rarely exceeding 12 inches, and produces four to eight brilliant orange-yellow flowers about 2 inches across with a heavy cinnamon scent. This plant is *a must for the beginning hobbyist.*

27

LYCASTE AROMATICA

LYCASTE DEPPEI

L. deppei is a larger plant that has flowers 4 inches across, green sepals dotted with brown-purple, petals white, lip yellow and flecked with red. An elegant flower that lasts seven to eight weeks on the plant.

L. skinneri, the most beautiful member of the family, has a white or blush pink flower 6 inches across. Semideciduous, the plants sometimes retain the foliage.

L. gigantea is a big plant with olive-green flowers about 6 to 7 inches across with a brown-edged lip fringed yellow. This species will require slightly warmer growing conditions than most Lycastes.

Grow the plants without direct sunshine until the bulbs are mature, then sun is needed. An airy position is best at all times. Pot Lycastes every second year after flowering, in 5- or 6-inch clay pots using a medium-grade fir bark or osmunda mixed with chopped tree fern. Fill pot with a generous amount of broken crocks because perfect drainage is essential.

Keep Lycastes evenly moist when in active growth but when the pseudobulbs have matured, water sparingly to encourage flower-spike initiation. After flowering, rest the plants completely with no water for seven to eight weeks. The majority of this genus are found at high altitudes indicating cool temperatures; I find they succeed well with 52 to 58 degrees F. at night in winter, with the exception of *L. gigantea.* Because of the folded nature of the foliage, avoid misting. Start your Lycaste collection with *L. aromatica* and *L. skinneri* for these are dependable plants.

Once in flower, Lycastes can be moved to any room in the house and will add an elegant note of decoration. I have never summered my plants outdoors but friends in the vicinity tell me they respond wonderfully. I keep my Lycastes at a south window in back of larger foliage orchids.

MILTONIA

Miltonia is a handsome genus of large-flowered epiphytes distributed through Costa Rica and Brazil with a great many from the Andes. The genus is divided into cool-growing and warm-growing varieties. However, even the heat-tolerant kinds need careful handling to survive a very hot summer. This genus requires more time and care than most orchids but the perfectly arranged bouquets of pansylike bloom are worth considerable effort. I have grown *Miltonia candida*, *M. roezlii*, and *M. spectabilis*, and have observed *M. cuneata*, *M. flavescens*, *M. regnellii*, and *M. vexillaria*. Some twenty species are known.

Mainly small plants, the Miltonias have elongated pseudobulbs tipped with several light green leaves. Even out of bloom, the plants are attractive. The flower spike is produced from the base of the most recently-formed pseudobulb and is erect, or sometimes arching, and carries either a solitary flower or many flowers. The inflorescence of the cool growers is white or pink blotched with crimson or magenta. The warm growers produce star-shaped yellow or white flowers marked purple or brown. There are many highly-colored hybrids available now.

M. flavescens from Brazil has bright yellow flowers, the lip marked yellow or white and blotched red-purple. This is a good Miltonia to start with since it will tolerate somewhat more heat than others in the genus.

M. spectabilis produces large solitary flowers with creamy-white sepals and petals, and a broad rose-purple lip thinly edged with pale rose or white. A very showy plant.

M. candida and *M. cuneata* produce 2- to 3-inch chestnut-brown flowers tipped with yellow.

M. regnellii has 3-inch white flowers blotched with rose at the base.

MILTONIA SPECTABILIS

M. roezlii bears two to five large white flowers, the lip scalloped and handsomely stained with yellow and splashed with red. This variety sometimes blooms twice a year and there are many hybrids available so color varies somewhat.

M. vexillaria has large white or rose flowers blotched with magenta. This species will tolerate more heat than others in the genus but still requires a cooler temperature after blossoming.

In summer, avoid growing Miltonias in direct sun but through the winter some dappled sunlight is beneficial. Repot every year in early spring or late fall in osmunda or fir bark mixed with chopped tree fern, and in small containers.

These epiphytes need moisture through the year but if you are without air conditioning, as I am, decrease watering somewhat during the very hot summer months. A small electric fan to help circulate air is a good idea too.

Many years ago, Miltonias were common house plants in England retaining their flowers for six to eight weeks in a cool area. You will find them most decorative plants.

MORMODES

Mormodes is an interesting genus of epiphytes found in Central America, Peru, and Mexico. Closely allied to the *Catasetum*, the plants produce unusual flowers in lurid color combinations. This group presents a real challenge, for basically they are difficult to grow but the inflorescence is well worth extra time and trouble. *Mormodes lineata, M. colossus, M. igneum,* and *M. buccinator* are but a few of the many members of this family. I have plants of all but the last.

The species in active growth is very decorative. The leaves, 12 to 14 inches tall, grow in a graceful fan from fleshy cigar-shaped pseudobulbs. Flower spikes are produced between the leaf axils as the foliage is shed. The many flowers last about three weeks. The erect spike are sometimes 2 to 3 feet high and more often than not when plants are in full flower the bulbs are bare, creating a bizarre effect. Generally winter flowering and oftentimes scented, the Mormodes deserve more attention from hobbyists.

M. lineata with pseudobulbs 5 to 10 inches long has flowers 1 inch across, yellow, shaded brown and streaked with orange-brown. The trumpet-shaped lip is twisted, and the inflorescence covered with short tiny hairs. The sassafras scent is extremely pleasing.

M. colossus is a slightly larger plant and produces 3-inch flowers of olive-green or yellow-brown, the lip brown and tan and narrowed at the base. The blossom resembles a bird in flight.

M. igneum is a beautiful species with small chocolate-brown flowers and an orange spotted lip that creates a hooded effect. A robust plant, this flowers freely.

M. buccinator, the most commonly grown plant of the genus, has pale yellow or green flowers spotted with crimson, the lip whitish.

Avoid growing Mormodes in strong direct sunshine; late afternoon sunlight is best. My plants remain at a west window all year. Although pot culture is satisfactory, I find cork bark or slabs of tree fern better, as this genus is highly intolerant of water on the pseudobulbs, at any time.

Through the growing season, these epiphytes require good moisture and humidity, but during the resting period they can't survive drying out like the Catasetums. Yet even the slightest overwatering at this time results in rotting of the bulbs. The best method seems to be to water lightly once a week and refrain from misting at all times.

Culture suggested for Mormodes often indicates warmth, 60 to 65 degrees F. at night in winter; yet I find my plants do better at slightly cooler temperatures of 52 to 58 degrees F. at night in winter.

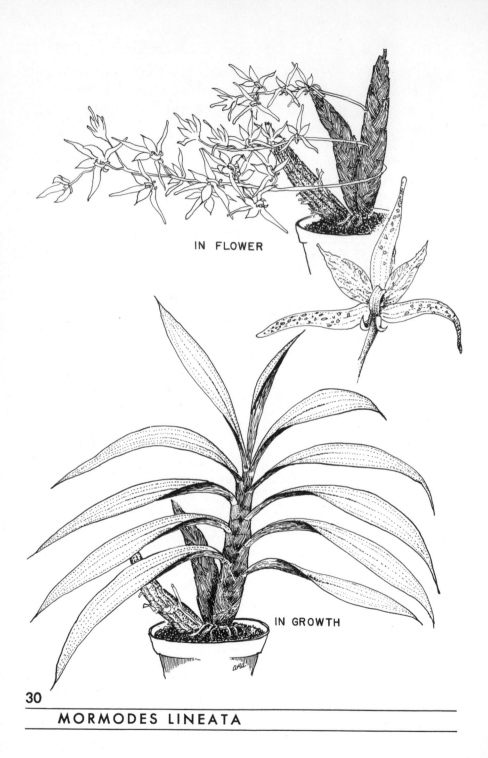

IN FLOWER

IN GROWTH

MORMODES LINEATA

NOTYLIA

Notylia, a genus of handsome miniature orchids from South America and Mexico, includes about fifteen species. They are still rather unknown in present-day collections but I believe we will soon see more of them. The tiny flowers, usually borne in tight clusters, are most pleasing. *Notylia xyphorous* does well placed close to the window; it is the only species easily obtained. *N. barkeri* is also pretty, but difficult to find.

The plants have either small short pseudobulbs with one leaf or are without pseudobulbs and have fleshy cactuslike fans of foliage. The spikes are usually pendant with many flowers varying in size from small to minute.

N. xyphorous with sharp, cactuslike 1-inch leaves has tiny, pale-purple flowers that appear in late summer for me.

N. barkeri produces white flowers spotted purple.

I grow my Notylias without much sun; they are suspended on pot hangers from a curtain rod in the corner of a window and grown close to the glass, where they get some late afternoon sun. In winter, the night temperature here is 58 degrees. They are on slabs of tree fern; excellent hosts for these miniatures. Even moisture is needed all year.

ODONTOGLOSSUM

Odontoglossum, a cool-growing genus of epiphytic orchids mainly from the Andes Mountains of Colombia produces some of the most beautiful flowers of all orchids. The delicate colors and frilled forms are a delight to the eye. Unfortunately these are difficult plants to grow for they require 45 to 55 degree F. temperatures all year, but where these conditions can be met, "Odonts" are certainly rewarding. *Odontoglossum citrosmum, O. grande, O. pulchellum, O. rossii,* and *O. uro-skinneri* are the only species in the genus I have grown successfully.

These orchids usually have flattened ovoid pseudobulbs sheathed with many small leaves and tipped with one or two larger leaves. The flower scapes are produced from the base or both sides of the last-made pseudobulb and carry one or several rather large flowers varying in color from white to yellow to pink to chestnut brown.

O. citrosmum is a pendulous variety that has fragrant frilly white flowers splotched with light pink or purple at the base of the lip. This fine orchid requires 50 to 56 degree coolness at night in winter.

O. grande, commonly called the Tiger Orchid, has large yellow flowers, 6 inches across and barred with brown.

O. pulchellum is a small plant about 14 inches tall with tiny white flowers delightfully scented.

4   Vivid yellow and chestnut brown *Odontoglossum grande* for late autumn into winter

O. rossii is a dwarf plant to about 8 inches and produces small white or rose flowers spotted maroon and with a broad scalloped lip.

O. uro-skinneri makes a handsome plant and is one of the few I imported from the jungle that survived. The large flowers have greenish sepals and petals marked with rich chestnut brown. The heartshaped lip is pink, broad, and marbled white. A very spectacular orchid.

Odontoglossums need light but not direct sun and a west window is perhaps the best location. Repotting is done in March or September in well-drained pots of fir bark mixed with shredded tree fern or in straight osmunda. Rather loose potting is a good idea. However, large pots of this genus can be carried over three to four years without damage to the plant. In fact, they seem to respond well when potbound.

These epiphytes require constant moisture, high humidity, good air circulation and temperatures of 45 to 58 degrees F. If you do not have air conditioning, you are more or less limited to the plants that I have grown for these seem to tolerate more heat than others in the genus. Although I have tried other species, I have never been successful under my conditions. Depending upon the species, watering should be slackened somewhat in the dull months after growth is completed.

ONCIDIUM

Oncidium is a large and varied genus of more than 700 epiphytic orchids distributed through Central America, Mexico, the West Indies, and parts of Brazil. Generally called spray orchids, the majority produce long spikes of beautiful yellow flowers marked with brown; they are welcome additions to any window collection. *Oncidium ampliatum, O. leucochilum, O. sarcodes, O. ornithorynchum, O. splendidum,* and *O. wentworthianum* are a few I have grown.

31

ODONTOGLOSSUM URO-SKINNERI

Many plants in the genus have compressed pseudobulbs tipped by one or two fleshy leaves; others are almost without pseudobulbs; and still others have pencil-like leaves. All are evergreen. The flower spike is generally produced from the base of the pseudobulb and in most cases is flexible and arching, sometimes 3 to 5 feet long. Flowers are small and numerous or large and few depending on the species. A great many bloom in autumn or winter and the flowers last a long time on the plant, often seven to nine weeks.

O. ampliatum with turtle-shaped pseudobulbs has small spray-type flowers of yellow and red-brown. When flowers fade, if the same spike is cut below the last node, the plant sometimes produces a second scape, as it did for me. Although the flowers were fewer and did not last too long, it was a pleasant surprise.

O. ornithorynchum grows about 14 inches tall and has hundreds of tiny lilac flowers. A very fine plant that will need

5   Yellow spray-type *Oncidium ampliatum* for spring or early summer

semishade and cool temperatures of 52 to 58 degrees F. at night in winter.

O. sarcodes is compact, 16 inches tall, and produces pretty scalloped yellow and chestnut-brown flowers.

O. splendidum, the most commonly grown, has solitary cactuslike leaves, 12 inches long, and vibrant yellow flowers barred with brown, the lip yellow, large and broad.

O. leucochilum has yellow-green flowers barred with brown.

O. wentworthianum bears flowers about an inch across of yellow blotched with brown. The above three species are excellent for window culture since they do not require as much direct sun as most in the genus.

Most Oncidiums need full sun for good flower production. The plants should be repotted every second year in well-drained containers of osmunda or fir bark mixed with chopped tree fern.

6   Lilac-colored, spray-type *Oncidium ornithorynchum* for fall and winter

ONCIDIUM SARCODES

While in active growth, these epiphytes require plenty of water and in most cases high humidity (50 to 70 percent). On completion of new growth a bone-dry rest of two to five weeks is essential. After flowers fade, another rest period of a few weeks is in order for most members in this genus. My Oncidiums have been grown under slightly cool conditions, 55 to 58 degrees F. at night in winter, but this family is so diversified that there are plants for many temperature ranges. *O. kramerianum* and *O. papilio* do well at 72 to 80 degrees; *O. cavendishianum* and *O. varicosum* need 52 to 60 degrees; *O. crispum* and *O. splendidum* thrive at 60 to 72 degrees.

Of a sun-loving nature, these epiphytes require summering outside. As house plants or as cut flowers, they are impossible to beat. The flower sprays sometimes last more than two months.

ORNITHOCEPHALUS

Ornithocephalus is a genus of desirable miniature orchids that tolerate some neglect and still bloom. One of my plants hidden behind some larger orchids survived beautifully without water for three months! These epiphytes from Central America also have the advantage of blossoming over a long period of time, perhaps three to four months. The tiny intricate flowers are green and white, and with most species, you will need a magnifying glass to really appreciate their beauty. *Ornithocephalus bicornis* and *O. inflexus* regularly produce flowers for me in early spring. *O. grandiflorus* is also handsome but difficult to find. There are about twenty-five species.

These plants, sometimes called Bird's Head Orchids, have fan-shaped fleshy foliage suggesting a cactus. The flower spikes push out from between the leaves and are usually slightly pendant carrying many flowers.

ORNITHOCEPHALUS GRANDIFLORUS (above)
POLYSTACHYA LUTEOLA (below)

O. bicornis, the most popular species, is 3 inches high and produces tiny greenish-white flowers.

O. inflexus has white flowers with a chartreuse lip.

O. grandiflorus has 5-inch leaves with 1-inch flowers, white with an emerald-green splotch at the base of the lip.

These orchids are grown out of direct sun and are repotted in sphagnum and fir bark every second year. They are tropical plants that adjust well to home temperatures of 58 to 62 F. at night, 72 to 80 during the day. Keep them evenly moist through the year.

PHAIUS

Phaius is a genus of large and showy terrestrial orchids originally from China, Africa, and Madagascar. These plants are eventually deciduous and will lose their leaves in the second year. Because the majority adapt to varying temperatures without difficulty, they are well suited to window culture. *Phaius grandifolius (tankervilliae)* and *P. maculatus* produce handsome flowers of unusual colors during the spring season.

Most species of this genus have short pseudobulbs hardly distinguishable and sheathed by the leaf bases. The leaves are often over 4 feet tall and the flower spikes are erect produced from the base of the pseudobulbs between the sheathing leaves. A healthy plant can produce ten to twenty large flowers sometimes 5 inches across that are long-lasting and scented.

P. grandifolius, which I have grown, is also known as *P. tankervilliae* and produces flowers that at first are pale in color; later they darken considerably and the sepals and petals are yellow-brown and silver-hued, the lip rose-purple and whitish with a blue spot in the center.

P. maculatus has a somewhat smaller inflorescence, buff yellow, lip marked with red on the front lobe. The dark green foliage is attractively spotted with yellow.

34

PHAIUS GRANDIFOLIUS

Phaius requires filtered sunlight rather than direct sun; a west exposure is good. Pot every second year in a compost of loam, manure, and osmunda, using 8- to 10-inch pots.

The genus requires watering and heavy feeding up to the actual opening of the flowers. Then a good rest is needed in a cooler temperature if possible. During the resting season, dry out the compost slightly and do not at any time mist the foliage.

Thrips, tiny wingless insects, are fond of this genus so check plants periodically. If they are infested, use a good all-around insecticide, such as DX aero spray bomb or Super-Cide (available at orchid-supply houses).

PHALAENOPSIS

Phalaenopsis, a genus of about seventy species of beautiful orchids from Java, Sumatra, Asia, and the Philippines, is commonly known as the Dogwood Orchid. The white flowers of the hybrids are popular for corsages and for cutting. The botanicals I grow have smaller and fewer flowers, but since plants rebloom again and again on old spikes it is rarely that I am without Phalaenopsis flowers. *Phalaenopsis amabilis*, *P. buyssoniana*, *P. esmeralda*, *P. lueddemanniana*, *P. mannii*, *P. rosea*, and *P. parishii* are the plants I have grown successfully, and there are many other fine species available in this worthwhile family.

The genus is characterized by absence of pseudobulbs, and it has short stems bearing three or more leathery leaves. Roots are mostly flat, often more than 2 feet long, winding in and around the pot and reaching into the air for moisture. Flower spikes are produced from leaf axils and are single or branched, short or extremely long.

P. amabilis is a large plant with leaves 20 inches long. It produces pure-white flowers, 5 inches across, spotted red.

P. buyssoniana, now known as *Doritis pulcherrima* var.

35

PHALAENOPSIS AMABILIS

buyssoniana, has mottled green leaves 5 to 8 inches long. The flowers are about 2 inches across; they are crimson-purple, the two lower sepals bordered with white.

P. *esmeralda* also known as *Doritis pulcherrima* has dark green leaves, 6 inches long, and bears delicate pink or rose flowers.

P. *lueddemanniana*, with leaves 6 to 10 inches long produces magnificent 2-inch flowers. They are white, barred amethyst-purple in a circular pattern.

P. *mannii* is a very handsome species with a golden-yellow inflorescence blotched with brown, the lip light yellow fringed purple. This one likes rather cool conditions, 54 to 62 degrees F.

P. *parishii* is a dwarf variety with leaves 2 to 4 inches long and white flowers spotted purple and overlayed with bright rose-purple; the fringed lip has a yellow-brown center.

P. *rosea*, a small plant with leaves about 8 inches long, has tiny white or rose flowers.

Phalaenopses thrive in a warm shady place, a curtained north window perhaps, with 50 to 70 percent humidity. Pot these epiphytes yearly in large-grade fir bark or in osmunda, and strive for perfect drainage. Night temperatures should never drop below 54 degrees.

Plants of this group grow through the year in compost that must never be dry; regular applications of liquid fertilizer promote healthy growth. After blossoming stops and flowers fade, snip off the stem just above a node on the same scape. Usually, another flower spike will be produced.

Flowers of Phalaenopses have amazing durability, lasting five to seven weeks on the plant. Cut and placed in a vase of water, their delicate simplicity is most charming in the home.

PHOLIDOTA

Pholidota, closely allied to the *Coelogyne* family, is a genus of orchids distributed through India, the Philippines, and

PHALAENOPSIS LUEDDEMANNIANA

China. The flowers are not showy but abundant and the plants thrive under home conditions. I have grown *Pholidota chinensis; P. articulata* is handsome, too.

The species have either decided pseudobulbs on a creeping rhizome or stemlike pseudobulbs. In most cases, scapes are erect and blossoming occurs at various times of year.

P. chinensis has small creamy-white flowers evenly spaced on a pendant scape. This plant blossoms in late summer for me.

P. articulata has 6-inch leaves and a pendant flower spike with a profusion of half-inch, yellowish-white flowers shaded green.

Pholidotas need semishade and slightly cool conditions so grow them close to a window with temperatures of 52 to 60 degrees F. at night in winter. Repot them every second year. I use small-grade fir bark but osmunda is satisfactory, too.

Pholidota imbricata, P. ventricosa and *P. conchoidea* are larger members of this family.

PLATYCLINIS

Platyclinis, a genus of about eight species, is chiefly native to the Philippines and includes some excellent miniature orchids. They are easy to grow and and the pendant spikes of small flowers are very decorative. *Platyclinis filiformis*, known as the Golden Chain orchid, is spectacular in bloom and I still grow this species. *P. uncata* is similar and *P. cornuta* is also desirable but not so showy.

These epiphytes have small pseudobulbs and narrow ever-green leaves. The flower spike comes from the top of the bulbs and is usually pendant carrying many flowers. A few species are sweet-scented.

P. cornuta has one leaf, 3 inches long, and a short scape. The inflorescence is white.

P. filiformis, also known as *Dendrochilum filiforme*, has 5-

PLATYCLINIS FILIFORMIS

to 6-inch grassy foliage and pendant chains of perfectly arranged, small yellow flowers in summer.

P. uncata produces slightly smaller yellow flowers.

Place these plants close to a window but not in direct sun. Redwood baskets are the best containers as perfect draimage is essential. Repot whenever the compost appears stale. Osmunda mixed with sphagnum moss is satisfactory.

Give these orchids plenty of water in the growing season but when growth has matured, water with discretion. Average home temperatures suit the genus.

PLEIONE

Pleione is a genus of about twenty species of spectacular terrestrial orchids that have been overlooked by hobbyists. Sometimes called Indian Crocus, these plants from China, Formosa, and Southeast Asia produce large, solitary, showy flowers. Plants are rather small and take time to adjust to home conditions but the blooms are well worth waiting for. *Pleione maculata* and *P. hookeriana* have blossomed for me. *P. pricei,* a young plant I bought two years ago is doing well and I hope for some flowers next year.

These deciduous plants have compressed cormlike pseudobulbs tipped with a few light green leaves that generally fall after bulbs mature. The short flower scapes are produced from the base of the pseudobulbs before, or along with, the new growth. Most species bear autumn flowers that last a week to ten days on the plant; many are scented.

P. maculata is about 12 inches tall and produces 4-inch white flowers. The white lip is streaked with purple inside and marked with dark red blotches on the margin. This species is a real beauty but it will take time and attention to bring it into flower.

P. hookeriana, with foliage about 5 inches high, produces leaves and flowers at the same time. They are rose-colored, almost purple, with a brown-purple splotch on the lip. Unlike most Pleiones, this species blossoms in spring.

P. pricei, with leaves about 6 inches high, bears a solitary 4-inch flower. It is pale rose with a large white-fringed lip.

Pleiones thrive at a west window where they receive diffused sunlight. Repotting is done yearly after flowering in a compost of sphagnum mixed with leaf mold and sand. Leave about half an inch of the top of the corms uncovered.

When they are first potted, water this genus with care. They are tricky in this respect, and it will take a great deal of guesswork to decide when root growth is really present. In the first month, I water them only once; in the fifth or sixth week, I increase waterings. When leaves have expanded fully, I slacken off moisture and eventually taper down to none. Flower spikes usually appear in autumn and then watering can be resumed.

These fine orchid plants need good air circulation and rather cool temperatures of 52 to 58 degrees F. at night in winter, so place them close to the window. In summer, they will tolerate higher daytime temperatures but still do better grown as cool as possible.

PLEUROTHALLIS

Pleurothallis is a genus of more than 500 species distributed through southern Florida, Mexico, Brazil, the Colombian Andes, and Costa Rica. They have only recently become popular. Many in the genus are excellent miniatures that grow well at a window. The intricate flowers appear at various times of year and last three to five weeks on the plant. *Pleurothallis barberiana*, *P. grobyi*, *P. ornata*, and *P. picta* are welcome additions to any collection.

These epiphytes are pseudobulbless plants. Some carry a solitary leaf on a slender stem; others are of tufted habit or the leaves are spaced on a creeping rhizome. The flower

38

PLEIONE PRICEI

spike comes from the base of the leaf and is arching or erect. Most species produce clusters of flowers; some, racemes of evenly-spaced blooms; others, flowers that rest on the leaf.

P. barberiana with 1-inch leaves produces slender nodding flower spikes crowded with white flowers spotted purple. This has been a dependable flowering orchid for me.

P. grobyi with 1- to 3-inch foliage bears small bright yellow flowers streaked with crimson.

P. ornata is a quaint species with 1-inch leaves and half-inch flowers of pale purple, the margins of the sepals fringed with white hairs.

P. picta, a densely tufted species with 2-inch leaves, bears yellow, sometimes orange, flowers half an inch across.

Diffused sunlight is best for Pleurothallis species with good air circulation and rather cool temperatures of 58 to 62 degrees F. at night in winter. These small plants need repotting about every other year in osmunda mixed with sphagnum moss. They should be watered daily when in active growth with less water in winter when they are resting. They are never left really dry.

POLYSTACHYA

Polystachya is a genus widely distributed through Africa, Asia, and America, the greater number of the 100 known species being small or miniature plants. The tiny cup-shaped flowers in a wide range of colors usually appear in the summer months. *Polystachya luteola* and *P. pubescens* are most commonly seen.

These epiphytes have short stems basally sheathed with leaves often thickened into small pseudobulbs that are tipped with two to three leaves. The flower spike is arching or erect and is produced from the apex of the bulbs.

P. luteola (Figure 33, page 103), a plant I grew for many

years, is 4 inches high with erect spikes bearing several yellow flowers shaded green; they are pleasantly scented.

P. pubescens has foliage about 6 inches long and pale yellow flowers streaked with red. They are charming.

Cultural data on this genus varies somewhat. The Polystachyas I grew successfully were given broken sunlight, average home temperatures, and water in moderation through the year. I believe many species in this genus will adapt to home conditions but I rarely see them advertised.

RENANTHERA

Renanthera, with about a dozen species, are epiphytic or terrestrial plants from China, the Philippines, Indonesia, and New Guinea, and a few are scattered through southeastern Asia. *Renanthera coccinea*, a towering plant, sometimes reaching 7 feet, is not for home culture but the dwarf species I have grown do make wonderful window-sill plants. These are *Renanthera imschootiana, R. annamensis*, and *R. pulchella*. The pretty red or yellow flowers are long-lasting and appear in spring or summer.

This genus is without pseudobulbs and has ascending stems of fleshy leaves with vinelike growth. The flower scape is produced from the leaf axils and carries ten or more flowers.

R. imschootiana rarely exceeds 20 inches and has vermilion flowers $2\frac{1}{2}$ inches across.

R. annamensis bears smaller flowers of yellow and crimson. *R. pulchella* produces yellow flowers blotched with red. These two plants may be a little difficult to locate but are worth a search.

The large Renantheras and its hybrids need full sun for good flower production; all day exposure is not too much. The dwarf species do well at my west windows with only afternoon sun. Potting is done every second year in fir bark mixed with sphagnum.

Plenty of water is necessary through the growing season, a decreased amount in winter. Temperatures of 55 to 64 degrees F. at night in winter will suit the dwarf species but the larger Renantheras will need more warmth.

RODRIGUEZIA

Rodriguezia is a small but charming genus of orchids from Brazil and Central America. They are dwarf plants with about twenty species known. Ideal for window culture, they producing intricate flowers in a wide range of cheerful colors. *Rodriguezia secunda* and *R. decora* are species that have always done well for me; *R. fragrans* is also worthwhile.

Most species in this genus have compressed pseudobulbs about 2 inches long, the remaining leaves sheathing the bulb. The arching spikes are produced from the base of the pseudobulb and carry many flowers about an inch long that appear in summer.

R. secunda, the most popular grown, has brilliant chains of rose-red flowers.

R. decora produces a slightly larger flower, white or rose spotted red; the spreading lip is usually white. This species does better on a raft or slab of tree fern because of the creeping rhizomes.

R. fragrans with small white flowers spotted yellow is scented.

Rodriguezia species thrive at a west window close to the glass with direct afternoon sunlight. Repot these plants every second year using osmunda or fir bark. Perfect drainage is necessary.

In active growth, these epiphytes will need copious watering and additional fertilizer. Even in winter, never allow the compost to become really dry.

I summer my plants on an open porch and since they are small orchids, I place them in back of some of the big foliage plants, where they thrive. When Rodriguezias bloom, I move them into the house for table decoration or place them on a kitchen window sill for color.

SCUTICARIA

Scuticaria is a genus of epiphytic orchids with only three known species. Although still rare, these strange plants from Brazil and Venezuela are available and bear magnificent, large, colorful flowers. I have grown *Scuticaria steelii* successfully; also *S. hadwenii*, but with less satisfaction. The plants bloom in late summer or early autumn and are desirable additions to any collection.

The species have short stemlike pseudobulbs tapering to pencil-like leaves sometimes *3 feet long*. The scape is short and grows from the side of the stem. It bears one to three long-lasting scented flowers.

S. steelii has light yellow, almost orange, flowers 4 inches across, spotted red. The waxen flower is very showy.

S. hadwenii produces a yellowish-green inflorescence blotched reddish brown.

Scuticarias are of notoriously poor appearance when not in flower because of the ropelike cactus foliage. This type leaf, if it can be called such, usually indicates full sun exposure. I find these plants prefer semishade. Because warmth and humidity are necessary, I set my plants far back from the window glass where the temperature is about 61 degrees F. at night in winter. They need liberal watering until growth is completed, but do not allow them to dry out completely in the dull months.

A slab of tree fern is a perfect host for these fine orchids; I do not recommend pot culture.

SCUTICARIA STEELII

SOPHRONITIS

Sophronitis is a genus of epiphytic orchids from Brazil with miniature species that rarely exceed 3 inches. Although not so easily grown as other miniature genera, Sophronitis is worth a try because most of the species bear brilliant red flowers. *Sophronitis grandiflora* has been in my collection for many years and I strongly recommend it. *S. cernua* is also very handsome and quite similar.

The species have small pseudobulbs that bear a solitary leathery leaf. The short scape comes from between bulb and leaf and carries only one flower, but there are usually many scapes.

S. grandiflora, sometimes called *S. coccinea*, produces a bright red flower almost 3 inches across.

S. cernua produces a smaller orange-red flower in the winter months.

Give these lovely orchids light but not sunshine and try to keep the plants as cool as possible at all times; hot summers will quickly kill them. Repot every second year in osmunda or small-grade fir bark and water liberally during growth. In the dull months, decrease the amount of water but don't allow the plants to become bone dry.

STANHOPEA

Stanhopea is a genus of more than twenty-five species native to Mexico, Peru, and Brazil. The unusual manner of flowering, from the base of the plant and the intricate structure of the inflorescence make these epiphytes a curiosity and perfect for hobbyists seeking the unusual. The large flowers in lurid color combinations are fascinating but last only a few days. My plants of *Stanhopea wardii*, *S. insignis*, and *S. oculata* always create a sensation when they bloom in August and September. *S. tigrina*, and *S. ecornuta* are other species of these easy-to-grow orchids.

Out of flower, the species in this genus look so much alike it is difficult to distinguish them and they are often sold under incorrect names. The pseudobulbs are oval, 2 to 3 inches long and bear a single, broad, dark green leaf 12 to 24 inches tall. The scape grows down and open orchid baskets or bottomless pots must be used. Flowers of many Stanhopeas are heavily scented, some having an odor of menthol or camphor; *S. tigrina* has a powerful vanilla fragrance.

S. wardii has yellow or white sepals and petals spotted red. The base of the complex lip is orange-yellow with a purple-brown spot on each side. (Flower color variable in this species.)

S. insignis has yellow flowers spotted purple with a white lip blotched lurid purple and a pair of fleshy horns.

S. oculata with a lemon-yellow inflorescence has a narrow orange-yellow lip darkly spotted. (Flower color variable in this species.)

S. tigrina bears the largest flowers in the genus, about 7 inches across, dull orange blotched purple with a yellow lip.

S. ecornuta produces cream-white flowers, yellow-orange in the center and spotted purple.

Stanhopeas should always be shaded. My plants are suspended on wire pot hangers from ceiling hooks in front of the north window where they receive light but no sun. I repotted them in tight-packed osmunda in redwood baskets when I bought them four years ago and they are still in the same containers. Occasionally I add some fresh osmunda pushing it in between the open slats. Most species in the genus react adversely to root disturbance so repot only when absolutely necessary. Large 10- to 12-inch baskets or bottomless pots are necessary.

This genus thrives in warmth. Night temperatures in winter should never drop below 60 degrees F. High humidity,

STANHOPEA OCULATA

7   Pendent flowering *Stanhopea wardii* for late summer into fall

about 70 percent, and abundant moisture are needed during growth. Additional fertilizer will be beneficial, too. In winter, decrease watering but never allow the compost to become really dry. It amazes me to see the great quantities of water these orchids require while in active growth.

STELIS

Stelis, a genus mainly of miniature orchids, includes some 500 species but few are known; they are from tropical America with a few native to Brazil and Peru. They produce very pretty flowers and once acclimated to home conditions are not difficult to grow. *Stelis ciliaris* and *S. micrantha* are welcome additions to any collection.

Most species have rhizome-like stems usually tipped with

a solitary oval leaf. The scape comes from the base of the leaf, or near there, and carries many small or tiny flowers of triangular form and are very appealing.

S. ciliaris is about 6 inches tall with many dark maroon or purple flowers. The margin of the sepals is usually fringed with hairs. The tiny flowers are very charming. This species bloomed only once for me for the second year I killed the plant by allowing the compost to become waterlogged.

S. micrantha is 6 inches high with small flowers. The sepals are yellow or greenish-white, the petals dark red. Usually this blossoms in autumn and is very pretty. I have been unable to locate a mature specimen.

Culture for the *Stelis* species varies according to the individual plant; in general, give them a shady spot near the window and even moisture all year. Repot Stelis only when absolutely necessary and strive for perfect drainage.

TRICHOPILIA

Trichopilia is a genus of epiphytic orchids fround in Mexico, Cuba, and Brazil. These plants, overlooked by hobbyists, produce large showy flowers. Although they are a little more difficult to grow than most orchids, I highly recommend them. Of the twenty-five species known, I have grown *Trichopilia suavis*, *T. tortilis*, *T. crispa*, *T. elegans*, and *T. marginata*.

The genus is characterized by flat compressed pseudobulbs tipped by a single fleshy leaf. The short scapes, erect or sometimes pendant, are produced from the base of the pseudobulbs and bear one to four flowers. Species bloom at various times of year but the majority of my plants come into flower in early spring or late summer.

T. suavis is about 14 inches tall and produces cream-white, 6-inch flowers spotted red. The trumpet-shaped lip is spotted pink and orange; the flower has a pleasing hawthorn scent.

41

TRICHOPILIA SUAVIS

T. tortilis is one of the first botanicals I grew. It has pale rose flowers about 6 inches across, the sepals and petals are twisted, almost of corkscrew shape, and the white scalloped lip is blotched red-brown. The pendant inflorescence against a red clay pot is extremely handsome.

T. crispa has large cherry-colored flowers with a crisped white lip spotted red.

T. marginata bears a rose-colored flower with a tubular lip marked inside with dark crimson. There are many varieties of this species and flower color differs somewhat.

T. elegans is unusual in the family because the flowers are much smaller, only about $1\frac{1}{2}$ inches long. They are white and retain the trumpet-shaped lip characteristic of this genus.

Trichopilias need light but not direct sun. My plants remain at a west window all year. Proper repotting is important for this genus which requires perfect drainage. Plants are intolerant of excess moisture at the roots. I use a little trick that may help you. When potting, put a thin layer of osmunda under the broken pot pieces. After a few waterings or in about six weeks, gently knock out the bottom of the pot with a hammer. The osmunda will keep the pot pieces and fir bark in place and the open base will provide extra air circulation. Repotting should be done yearly, immediately after flowering.

This group requires careful watering even while in active growth. I soak plants once a week from March through November, the rest of the year, only once every three weeks. Mostly cool growing, night temperatures of 52 to 58 degrees F. in winter will suit Trichopilias. Grow them as cool as possible in summer.

VANDA

Vanda is a genus of epiphytic orchids native to the Far East, Malaya, the Philippines, and East Indies. Many hybrids are grown with great success in warmer countries, such as

Hawaii and southern Florida. Vandas, closely allied to Aerides and Renantheras, need warmth and many hours of
direct sun. Of the seventy species known, most are easy to
grow and produce large showy flowers where temperate
conditions prevail all year. However, *Vanda coerulea*, which
I have grown successfully, will tolerate cooler temperatures
and needs less sun so I recommend this species for the beginner. *Vanda teres* and *V. suavis* are worthwhile but they
have never responded for me.

Plant stems grow to great heights, and it is advisable to
select a mature plant about 3 feet tall. Most of the species
have leathery leaves in fan formation and arching flower
spikes that are produced from between the leaves. A healthy
plant will have several spikes.

V. coerulea bears pale-blue flowers veined darker blue.
They are about 4 inches across and appear in late fall.

V. teres has fleshy pencil-like foliage. Flowers are pale rose
or magenta. This species needs a decided rest in winter.

V. suavis with cream-white flowers spotted red-purple is
very free flowering. There are many hybrids so flower color
varies considerably.

Vandas *must have* at least six hours of direct sun to produce flowers. Repotting should be done infrequently and
large containers, about 8 to 12 inches, are best. Various com-
posts have been used for this family but straight osmunda is
always satisfactory.

Here in the Midwest where winters can be very gray, it
always delights me to see a fine collection of Vandas in bloom,
and they are quite rare. Apparently the winter sunlight is just
not intense enough for these wonderful orchids.

In addition to the eight orchid genera discussed that are
predominately composed of miniature plants (*Notylia, Orni-*

thocephalus, Platyclinis, Pleurothallis, Polystachya, Rodrigue-
zia, Sophronitis, Stelis), the more popular genera also contain
some very small orchids that are most attractive.

CATTLEYA

C. walkeriana with about 6-inch foliage produces a large,
rose-colored flower.

DENDROBIUM

D. jenkinsii grows 2 inches tall and has golden-yellow
flowers.

D. loddigesii with 6-inch foliage bears a solitary 1-inch
rose-colored flower.

D. monile grows to 6 inches and has pairs of pure white,
fragrant flowers.

EPIDENDRUM

E. matthewsii is 2 inches tall, and the small flowers are
purplish.

E. odoratissimum has 6-inch foliage with small, yellowish-
green or white flowers on an erect spike.

E. schlecterianum, a curious plant with small fleshy green
leaves, has pale greenish-yellow flowers tinged pink.

LAELIA

L. rubescens has white or rose flowers with a dark maroon
spot at the base of the lip. Plants grow to about 6 inches.

ODONTOGLOSSUM

O. cervantesii is about 6 inches high with drooping scapes of scented pale-pink flowers.

O. krameri is 6 to 7 inches high; the flowers are violet.

ONCIDIUM

O. limminghi has a creeping growth habit with 1- to 2-inch leaves. The ochre flowers are very pretty.

O. suttoni with 3- to 4-inch leaves bears yellow-and-brown flowers.

O. caminophorum is 6 inches high with yellow and chestnut-brown flowers.

These are but a few of the many miniature orchids available, and more species are being discovered every day. I have found that these small plants take longer to adjust to the new environment of a home than other orchids, but, once established, are dependable plants. When buying miniatures, ask for them by their full name—genus and species.

APPENDIX

ORCHID CHART FOR QUICK REFERENCE

Direct Sunshine

FULL SUN: 6 *to* 8 hours　　BROKEN SUN: 2 *to* 3 hours

HALF-SUN: 3 *to* 4 hours　　SEMISHADE: 1 *to* 2 hours

SHADE: light, no sun

* *Terrestrial*　　† *Deciduous*　　‡ *Semi-terrestrial*

NAME	PLANT SIZE INCHES	FLOWER COLOR	FLOWER SIZE INCHES	TIME OF BLOOM	SUGGESTED EXPOSURE
AERIDES					
crassifolium	7-12	amethyst purple	1-2	summer	half-sun
fieldingii	24-40	white mottled with purple	1½	various	full sun
japonicum	3-5	white marked red	1	summer	half-sun
maculosum	7-10	pale rose spotted purple	1	summer	half-sun
multiflorum	9-18	deep rose	1	summer	half-sun
odoratum	12-40	creamy white	1	various	full sun
ASPASIA					
epidendroides	9-15	greenish with chocolate brown	2-2½	summer, spring	semishade
lunata	9-15	green and white marked brown	2-3	early spring	semishade
odorata	6-14	white marked brown	3	spring	semishade
principissa	8-26	greenish with chocolate brown	3	various	semishade
BIFRENARIA					
harrisoniae	11-16	cream white with yellow lip marked purple	3	spring	half-sun
tyrianthina	11-20	reddish purple	3	spring	half-sun
BLETIA					
*†catenulata	30-36	rose purple	1	summer	half-sun
*†purpurea	40-48	rose	1	summer	half-sun
*†shepherdii	24-36	rose-purple	1-2	summer	half-sun
*†sherrattiana	36-48	rose-purple	1-2	summer	half-sun
BRASSAVOLA					
cucullata	5-7	white, spotted red	2-4	various	full sun
digbyana	8-15	greenish white	5-7	various	full sun
glauca	5-12	greenish white	3	spring	half-sun
nodosa	6-9	white, spotted red	2-4	various	full snu
BRASSIA					
caudata	16-24	light green tinted yellow, spotted brown	5-8 (long)	various	full sun

NAME	PLANT SIZE INCHES	FLOWER COLOR	FLOWER SIZE INCHES	TIME OF BLOOM	SUGGESTED EXPOSURE
gireoudiana	8-16	yellow and brown	5-7 (long)	various	full sun
maculata	15-22	greenish yellow, spotted brown	6-9 (long)	summer	full sun
BULBOPHYLLUM barbigerum	3-5	greenish yellow with purple black hairs	1	summer	half-sun
careyanum	5-7	variable in color, usually reddish brown	½	summer	half-sun
lemniscatoides	3-5	dark purple	½	various	half-sun
lobbii	7-9	buff yellow, almost copper color	2-4	summer	broken sun
macranthum	4-7	red splashed with yellow	½	various	half-sun
virescens	10-20	light green, shaded yellow	1-3	various	half-sun
CALANTHE *biloba	12-18	purple tinted yellow brown	1	summer	broken sun
*†labrosa	10-15	rose-purple	½-1	winter	broken sun
*masuca	20-30	dark violet	1	summer	broken sun
*†rosea	10-14	variable; white to dark rose	1	winter	half-sun
*†vestita	10-14	cream white or pink shades	1	winter	half-sun
*veratrifolia	20-30	variable, usually white	2	various	half-sun
CATASETUM †pileatum	9-14	ivory white	3	autumn	half-sun until growth matures; then, full sun
†russellianum	9-12	pale green, veined dark green	2-3	summer, autumn	half-sun until growth matures; then, full sun
†scurra	4-7	cream white	1	early spring	half-sun until growth matures; then full sun
†viridiflavum	8-14	variable; usually pale green and yellow	2-3	late summer	half-sun until growth matures; then, full sun
CATTLEYA aclandiae	6-10	olive green, blotched purple	3-4	summer	full sun or half-sun
citrina	6-10	bright yellow with white lip	2-3	spring, summer	full sun or half-sun
dolosa	8-10	rose magenta	3	autumn	half-sun
forbesii	12-16	greenish yellow	3-4	various	half-sun
nobilior	6-11	rose magenta	3-4	various	half-sun
luteola	5-9	pale yellow streaked purple	2	summer	half-sun
skinneri	12-26	rose-purple	2-3	spring	full sun
CHYSIS †aurea	12-20	yellow marked red	3	various	half-sun

NAME	PLANT SIZE INCHES	FLOWER COLOR	FLOWER SIZE INCHES	TIME OF BLOOM	SUGGESTED EXPOSURE
†bractescens	14-28	waxy white	3-4	spring	half-sun
†laevis	14-20	yellow-orange	2	spring	half-sun
CIRRHOPETALUM					
cumingii	3-5	red-purple	1½ (long)	various	broken sun
longisimmum	5-7	pink or buff	6-12 (long)	winter	broken sun
mastersianum	5-7	pale orange	2 (long)	autumn	broken sun
ornatissimum	4-6	yellow-purple suffused brown	5 (long)	usually autumn	broken sun
COELOGYNE					
cristata	7-12	white	3-4	winter, spring	semishade
flaccida	11-15	white, almost buff with faint red lip	1½	winter, spring	shade
fuscescens	9-15	greenish brown	1½	winter	shade
gardneriana	9-16	white with yellow marked brown	1-2	winter	shade
massangeana	12-30	sepals and petals ochre, lip, brown	2½	various	semishade
meyeriana	10-18	green, lip marked black	2	late summer	semishade
ochracea	8-12	white marked orange	1	spring, summer	half-sun
pandurata	14-32	green, veined black	4	summer	half-sun
speciosa alba	10-14	creamy beige	3-4	various	semishade
CYCNOCHES					
†chlorochilon	10-26	yellow-green with cream lip	5	various	half-sun
†egertonianum	10-20	green suffused with purple	1½	summer	half-sun
CYPRIPEDIUM	*leaf spread*				
‡bellatulum	9-12	white or pale yellow marked with maroon	2-3	various	semishade
‡concolor	6-8	yellow with crimson dots	2-3	summer	semishade
‡insigne	8-12	apple green, veined brown	4-5	various	semishade
‡niveum	6-8	white, dotted purple	3-4	summer	semishade
DENDROBIUM	*Plant size*				
aggregatum	4-8	vivid yellow	1	spring	full sun
chrysotoxum	12-30	white with orange lip	1-2	early spring	full sun
dalhousieanum	24-72	tawny yellow and rose, lip marked crimson	3-4	spring	half-sun
densiflorum	20-36	orange yellow	1-2	spring	full sun
†fimbriatum	20-38	orange yellow	2-3	various	half-sun
jamesianum	12-20	white with yellow-red throat	4-5	spring	half-sun

NAME	PLANT SIZE INCHES	FLOWER COLOR	FLOWER SIZE INCHES	TIME OF BLOOM	SUGGESTED EXPOSURE
†nobile hybrids	12-36	usually blush white with lavender tips and lip	3-4	winter spring	half-sun in growth; full sun when leaves fall
phalaenopsis	12-36	lavender	2-4	various	full sun
†pierardii	18-72	pale lavender	2-3	spring	half-sun
†superbum	24-72	lavender	4-5	winter, spring	half-sun in growth; full sun when leaves fall
thyrsiflorum	14-30	white with orange lip	1½-2	spring	half-sun
†wardianum	24-30	white tipped purple	2-3	winter, spring	half-sun
EPIDENDRUM					
aromaticum	14-18	greenish yellow	½-1	spring	full sun
atropurpureum	14-18	greenish purple and chocolate brown	1-2	early spring	full sun
elegans	12-18	dark rose	2	winter	half-sun
nocturnum	10-16	greenish white	3-4	winter	half-sun
‡o'brienianum	24-62	red or pink or orange	1	various	half-sun
prismatocarpum	18-32	vivid yellow blotched purple	2-3	summer	full sun
stamfordianum	15-18	yellow spotted red	1	early spring	half-sun
vitellinum	7-12	cinnabar red	1	winter	broken sun
GONGORA					
armeniaca	10-14	apricot yellow	1½	late summer	broken sun
galeata	8-10	yellow	1½	various	broken sun
HEXISEA					
bidentata	6-20	red	1	spring, summer	half-sun
LAELIA					
autumnalis	7-12	rose purple	3-4	late autumn	full sun
flava	6-10	canary yellow	1½	various	half-sun
pumila	5-9	rose	2-3	summer, autumn	half-sun
superbiens	36-48	rose and purple streaked	5-6	winter	full sun
LOCKHARTIA					
acuta	6-10	yellow, marked red	½-1	mostly summer	semishade
lunifera	12-16	yellow and red	½-1	summer	half-sun
oerstedii	18-24	yellow, marked red	½-1	summer	semishade
LYCASTE					
†aromatica	10-16	yellow	2	winter	broken sun in growth; semishade when leaves fall

NAME	PLANT SIZE INCHES	FLOWER COLOR	FLOWER SIZE INCHES	TIME OF BLOOM	SUGGESTED EXPOSURE
†deppei	16-24	greenish brown spotted red	5	mostly winter	broken sun in growth; semi-shade when leaves fall
†gigantea	20-30	olive green	6-7	various	
skinneri	15-24	whitish rose	6	various	broken sun
MILTONIA					
candida	10-20	sepals and petals reddish brown with white lip	3	autumn	broken sun
cuneata	10-15	sepals and petals chestnut brown tipped yellow	3	spring	broken sun
flavescens	14-18	yellow and red		summer	broken sun
regnellii	10-18	sepals and petals white or rose with white lip	2-3	various	broken sun
roezlii	12-15	white with purple blotch	3	spring, autumn	broken sun
spectabilis	8-12	rose colored with purple lip	3	summer	half-sun
vexillaria	9-15	usually rose	3	spring	half-sun
MORMODES					
†buccinator	13-20	sepals and petals pale green to buff, lip, white	4	autumn	half-sun in growth; broken sun when leaves fall
†colossus	23-30	sepals and petals olive green or yellow with brown or yellow lip	5-6	autumn, winter	half-sun in growth; broken sun when leaves fall
†igneum	18-24	reddish brown with orange lip	3-4	winter	half-sun in growth; broken sun when leaves fall
†lineata	13-20	yellow striped orange brown	1	winter	half-sun in growth; broken sun when leaves fall
ODONTOGLOSSUM					
citrosmum	14-20	white or pink	3	various	semishade
grande	10-16	yellow barred chestnut brown	5-7	winter	semishade
pulchellum	10-14	white	½-1	spring	broken sun
rossii	4-6	white spotted dark brown	1-2	various	broken sun
uro-skinneri	12-20	sepals and petals greenish marked with brown, lip, pink	1-2	spring	half-sun
ONCIDIUM					
ampliatum	10-14	bright yellow, spotted red	1	early spring	full sun
leucochilum	10-20	yellow green, barred brown	1-2	various	half-sun

NAME	PLANT SIZE INCHES	FLOWER COLOR	FLOWER SIZE INCHES	TIME OF BLOOM	SUGGESTED EXPOSURE
ornithorynchum	8-20	rose lilac	½-1	autumn, winter	half-sun
sarcodes	10-16	chestnut brown and vivid yellow	1	various	broken sun
splendidum	12-18	yellow barred brown	1½-2	winter, spring	half-sun
wentworthianum	12-20	yellow and brown	1	various	half-sun
PHAIUS					
*†grandifolius	22-40	brown and white	4	spring, summer	broken sun or semishade
*†maculatus	22-40	buff-yellow marked brown	3	spring	broken sun or semishade
PHALAENOPSIS	*leaf spread*				
amabilis	8-24	white	3-4	winter	semishade
buyssoniana	5-9	crimson purple and white	1½	summer	semishade
esmeralda	4-7	pink or lavender	1	various	semishade
lueddemanniana	6-12	white heavily barred with amethyst purple	1½-2	various	semishade
parishii	2-5	white with rose purple	½-1	summer	semishade
mannii	7-8	golden yellow, barred brown	1	various	semishade
rosea	4-8	white with rose purple	1½	various	semishade
PLEIONE					
*†hookeriana	5-6	rose-purple	3	spring	broken sun
*†maculata	10-12	white with white lip streaked purple	2	late autumn	broken sun
*†pricei	5-6	pale rose	4	spring	broken sun
RENANTHERA					
annamensis	8-28	sepals and petals yellow, spotted red	1½	summer	semishade
imschootiana	8-30	orange-red	2-2½	spring, summer	semishade
pulchella	6-16	yellow and red	1-2	summer	full sun
RODRIGUEZIA					
decora	8-20	white or rose, spotted red	1½	summer	half-sun
fragrans	8-14	white	1	summer	half-sun
secunda	8-12	red	1½	summer	half-sun
SCUTICARIA					
hadwenii	9-20	yellowish green, spotted with chestnut brown	2-3	various	semishade
steelii	24-48	light yellow, spotted orange	3	various	semishade
SOPHRONITIS					
cernua	3-4	red	2-3	winter	semishade
grandiflora	3	red	2-3	winter	semishade

NAME	PLANT SIZE INCHES	FLOWER COLOR	FLOWER SIZE INCHES	TIME OF BLOOM	SUGGESTED EXPOSURE
STANHOPEA					
ecornuta	24-36	white, spotted purple	5-7	summer	shade
insignis	24-36	yellow, spotted purple	5-7	summer	shade
oculata	24-36	lemon-yellow, spotted black	5-7	summer	shade
tigrina	24-36	orange, blotched with purple	7-8	summer, autumn	shade
wardii	24-36	yellow or white, spotted purple	5-6	summer	shade
TRICHOPILIA					
crispa	8-14	cherry colored, white lip	3-5	spring, summer	half-sun
elegans	7-12	white	2	spring, summer	half-sun
marginata	6-10	pink	5	spring, summer	half-sun
suavis	8-16	white, spotted red, lip, pink, spotted orange	6	spring, summer	half-sun
tortilis	8-12	whitish pink, white lip	5	spring, summer	half-sun
VANDA					
coerulea	36-60	pale blue	4	autumn, winter	full sun
teres	36-60	pale rose	4	various	full sun
suavis	36-60	white, spotted red	4	various	full sun
MINIATURE SPECIES OF POPULAR GENERA					
CATTLEYA					
walkeriana	5-6	rose	3-5	winter	half-sun
DENDROBIUM					
jenkinsii	1-3	golden yellow	1	spring	half-sun
loddigesi	5-6	rose	1	spring	half-sun
monile	5-6	white	1	various	half-sun
EPIDENDRUM					
matthewsii	2	purple	$\frac{3}{4}$	various	half-sun
odoratissimum	5-6	yellow-green or white	$\frac{3}{4}$	various	half-sun
schlecterianum	1	greenish yellow, tinged pink	$\frac{1}{2}$	various	half-sun
LAELIA					
rubescens	5-8	white or rose	1-2	winter	full sun
ODONTOGLOSSUM					
cervantesii	6-7	pale pink	1-2	usually spring	half-sun
krameri	6-7	violet	1-2	various	semishade
ONCIDIUM					
caminophorum	5-6	yellow and brown	$\frac{1}{2}$-1	various	half-sun
limminghii	1-2	yellow or ochre, spotted red	1	summer	full sun
suttonii	3-4	yellow and brown	1	various	half-sun

◇◇◇◇◇
Aspasia epidendroides; A, principissa
Bletia purpurea
Brassavola cucullata; B. nodosa
Brassia caudata; B. gireoudiana; B. maculata
Bulbophyllum barbigerum; B. lobbii
Calanthe rosea; C. vestita
Catasetum russellianum; C. scurra
Cattleya citrina, C. forbesii
Chysis bractescens, C. laevis
Cirrhopetalum cumingii
Coelogyne cristata; C. massangeana; C. meyeriana; C. ochracea
Cycnoches chlorichilon
Cypripedium concolor; C. insigne
Dendrobium aggregatum; D. nobile and hybrids; D. pierardii;
    D. thyrsiflorum
Epidendrum aromaticum; E. atropurpureum; E. fragrans;
    E. o'brienianum
Gongora armeniaca; G. galeata
Hexisea bidentata
Lockhartia oerstedii
Lycaste aromatica; L. deppei; L. skinneri
Miltonia candida; M. spectabilis
Mormodes lineata
Notylia xyphorous
Odontoglossum grande; O. pulchellum
Oncidium ampliatum; O. sarcodes; O. splendidum
Ornithocephulus bicornis; O. inflexus
Phaius grandifolius
Phaleanopsis amabilis; P. csmeralda; P. rosea
Pholidota chinensis
Platyclinis filiformis
Pleurothallis grobyi
Renanthera imschootiana
Rodriguezia decora; R. fragrans; R. secunda
Sophronitis grandiflora
Stanhopea oculata; S. wardii
Trichopilia elegans; T. suavis; T. tortilis

ORCHID FLOWERS BY COLOR

WHITE
Aerides odoratum
Bifrenaria harrisoniae
Brassavola glauca
Brassavola nodosa
Catasetum scurra
Chysis bractescens
Coelogyne cristata
Coelogyne ochracea
Cypripedium niveum
Odontoglossum pulchellum
Phalaenopsis amabilis
Trichopilia elegans

YELLOW
Dendrobium aggregatum
Dendrobium chrysotoxum
Epidendrum prismatocarpum
Epidendrum stamfordianum
Gongora armeniaca
Gongora maculata
Laelia flava
Lockhartia acuta
Lockhartia oerstedii
Oncidium ampliatum
Oncidium splendidum

LAVENDER
Bletia purpurea
Cattleya skinneri
Dendrobium pierardii
Dendrobium superbum
Laelia pumila
Laelia superbiens
Oncidium ornithorynchum
Phalaenopsis esmeralda
Phalaenopsis rosea
Pleione hookeriana

RED
Epidendrum vitellinum
Epidendrum o'brienianum
Hexisea bidentata
Renanthera imschootiana
Rodriguezia secunda
Sophronitis grandiflora

ORCHID FLOWERS BY SEASONS

ORCHID TYPES

SINGLE-FLOWERED ORCHIDS

(*Produce one flower to a stem but sometimes there are two or more stems in bloom at the same time.*)

Cattleya citrina
Huntleya meleagris
Laelia pumila
Lycaste aromatica
Lycaste deppei
Lycaste gigantea
Lycaste skinneri
Miltonia spectabilis
Pleione hookeriana
Pleione maculata
Scuticaria steelii
Sophronitis grandiflora

CLUSTER-FLOWERING ORCHIDS

Aspasia principissa
Bifrenaria harrisoniae
Brassavola glauca
Cattleya skinneri
Chysis aurea
Chysis bractescens
Coelogyne cristata
Dendrobium chrysotoxum
Dendrobium thyrsiflorum
Epidendrum o'brienianum
Hexisea bidentata
Laelia superbiens
Phaius grandifolius

SPRAY-ORCHIDS

Calanthe vestita
Dendrobium aggregatum
Epidendrum aromaticum
Epidendrum atropurpureum
Epidendrum stamfordianum
Mormodes igneum
Mormodes lineata
Odontoglossum uro-skinneri
Oncidium ampliatum
Oncidium leucochilum
Oncidium ornithorynchum
Oncidium sarcodes
Oncidium splendidum
Oncidium wentworthianum
Phalaenopsis amabilis
Renanthera imschootiana
Vanda coerulea

PENDANT-ORCHIDS

Aerides crassifolium
Aerides multiflorum
Aerides odoratum
Brassia maculata
Catasetum russellianum
Coelogyne citrosmum
Coelogyne massangeana
Cycnoches egertonianum
Dendrobium pierardii
Dendrobium superbum
Gongora armeniaca
Gongora maculata
Rodriguezia secunda

PLANT LOCATION

ORCHIDS FOR A
WARM LOCATION

Aerides fieldingii
Aerides odoratum
Brassia maculata
Cattleya skinneri
Coelogyne pandurata
Dendrobium chrysotoxum
Oncidium splendidum
Phalaenopsis amabilis
Stanhopea oculata
Stanhopea tigrina
Stanhopea wardii
Vanda suavis
Vanda teres

ORCHIDS FOR A
COLD LOCATION

Cattleya citrina
Coelogyne cristata
Coelogyne flaccida
Cypripedium fairrieanum
Cypripedium villosum
Epidendrum vitellinum
Laelia autumnalis
Laelia superbiens
Miltonia vexillaria
Odontoglossum grande
Odontoglossum pulchellum
Odontoglossum uro-skinneri
Pleione hookeriana
Pleione maculata
Sophronitis grandiflora
Vanda coerulea

ORCHIDS FOR
FULL SUN

Aerides fieldingii
Aerides odoratum
Brassavola cucullata
Brassavola digbyana
Brassavola nodosa
Brassia maculata
Dendrobium aggregatum
Dendrobium chrysotoxum
Epidendrum aromaticum
Epidendrum atropurpureum
Epidendrum prismatocarpum
Hexisea bidentata
Laelia superbiens
Oncidium ampliatum
Vanda suavis
Vanda teres

ORCHIDS FOR A
SHADED WINDOW

Coelogyne cristata
Coelogyne flaccida
Coelogyne gardneriana
Coelogyne massangeana
Cypripedium bellatum
Cypripedium insigne
Epidendrum vitellinum
Lockhartia oerstedii
Odontoglossum grande
Phalaenopsis amabilis
Phalaenopsis lueddemanniana
Scuticaria steelii
Sophronitis grandiflora
Stanhopea oculata
Stanhopea tigrina
Stanhopea wardii

SOURCES OF ORCHID PLANTS & SUPPLIES

Alberts & Merkel Bros., Inc.
P.O. Box 537
Boynton Beach, Florida 33435

Very fine catalog; many botanical and miniature orchids

Fennell Orchid Co.
26715 S.W. 157th Avenue
Homestead, Florida 33030

Excellent informative catalog with many hard-to-find species

Fuchs Orchids
Box 113
Naranja, Florida 33030

Fine stock of species; lists available

Hausermann's Orchids
Box 363
Elmhurst, Illinois 60126

Listings available; good source for many unusual species

S. M. Howard Orchids
11802 Huston Street
North Hollywood, California
  91607

Large assortment of botanicals and hard-to-find orchids

Gordon M. Hoyt Orchids
Seattle Heights, Washington
  98063

Excellent source for Miltonias, Odontoglossums, and allied cool-growing genera; catalog

Margaret Ilgenfritz Orchids
Monroe, Michigan 48161

Informative catalog on botanicals; good source of unusual species

Jones & Scully, Inc.
2200 N.W. 33rd Avenue
Miami, Florida 33142

Very fine house for orchids of all types; color catalog

Oscar M. Kirsch
2869 Oahu Avenue
Honolulu, Hawaii 96822

Lager & Hurrell Orchids
426 Morris Avenue
Summit, New Jersey 07901

Fine catalog of botanicals; an excellent source

Rod McLellan
1450 El Camino Real
S. San Francisco, California
  94080

Listings of botanicals

Rivermont Orchids
Signal Mountain, Tennessee
  37377

Listings of hard-to-find botanicals

Fred A. Stewart Co.
Box 307
San Gabriel, California 91778

Catalog; very fine Cattleya hybrids

FOREIGN

Bangkrabue Nursery
15 Klahoms Lane Bangkrabue
Bangkok, Thailand

Corona Florists
237 Orchard Road
Singapore 9

Large listings of Vandas and Dendrobiums

H. A. Dunn Orchids
Box 1077
Balboa, Canal Zone

Listings of many unusual botanicals

Orquideario Catarinerse
P.O. Box 1
Corupa
Santa Catarina, Brazil

Catalog

Orquideas Mexicanas, S.A.
Ave. Tiro Al Pichon #148
P.O. Box 23738
Mexico 10, D.F. Mexico

All types of Mexican genera plants

Index